# HANDS-ON PYTHON **PROGRAMMING** FOR BEGINNERS

LEARN PRACTICAL PYTHON FAST



AI PUBLISHING

First Printing, 2021

Edited by AI Publishing
eBook Converted and Cover by Gazler Studio
Published by AI Publishing LLC

ISBN-13: 978-1-7347901-9-1

# How to Contact Us

If you have any feedback, please let us know
by sending an email to contact@aipublishing.io.

Your feedback is immensely valued,
and we look forward to hearing from you.
It will be beneficial for us
to improve the quality of our books.

To get the Python codes and materials used in this book,
please click the link below:

www.aipublishing.io/book-hands-on-python

The order number is required

# About the Publisher

At AI Publishing Company, we have established an international learning platform specifically for young students, beginners, small enterprises, startups, and managers who are new to data science and artificial intelligence.

Through our interactive, coherent, and practical books and courses, we help beginners learn skills that are crucial to developing AI and data science projects.

Our courses and books range from basic introduction courses to language programming and data science to advanced courses for machine learning, deep learning, computer vision, big data, and much more. The programming languages used include Python, R, and some data science and AI software.

AI Publishing's core focus is to enable our learners to create and try proactive solutions for digital problems by leveraging the power of AI and data science to the maximum extent.

Moreover, we offer specialized assistance in the form of our online content and eBooks, providing up-to-date and useful insight into AI practices and data science subjects, along with eliminating the doubts and misconceptions about AI and programming.

Our experts have cautiously developed our contents and kept them concise, short, and comprehensive so that you can understand everything clearly and effectively and start practicing the applications right away.

We also offer consultancy and corporate training in AI and data science for enterprises so that their staff can navigate through the workflow efficiently.

With AI Publishing, you can always stay closer to the innovative world of AI and data science.

If you are eager to learn the A to Z of AI and data science but have no clue where to start, AI Publishing is the finest place to go.

Please contact us by email at
contact@aipublishing.io.

# AI Publishing is Looking for Authors Like You

**An Important Note to Our Valued Readers:**

# Download the Color Images

Our print edition books are available only in black & white at present. However, the digital edition of our books is available in color PDF.

We request you to download the PDF file containing the color images of the screenshots/diagrams used in this book here:

www.aipublishing.io/book-hands-on-python

The typesetting and publishing costs for a color edition are prohibitive. These costs would push the final price of each book to $50, which would make the book less accessible for most beginners.

We are a small company, and we are negotiating with major publishers for a reduction in the publishing price. We are hopeful of a positive outcome sometime soon. In the meantime, we request you to help us with your wholehearted support, feedback, and review.

For the present, we have decided to print all of our books in black & white and provide access to the color version in PDF. This is a decision that would benefit the majority of our readers, as most of them are students. This would also allow beginners to afford our books.

# Get in Touch with Us

Feedback from our readers is always welcome.

For general feedback, please send us an email at
contact@aipublishing.io
and mention the book title in the subject line.

Although we have taken extraordinary care to ensure the accuracy of our content, errors do occur. If you have found an error in this book, we would be grateful if you could report this to us as soon as you can.

If you are interested in becoming an AI Publishing author and if you have expertise in a topic and you are interested in either writing or contributing to a book, please send us an email at
author@aipublishing.io.

# Table of Contents

# Preface

If you are reading these lines, you are probably one of those people who are either absolute beginners to programming or are familiar with some programming language other than Python. If you fall in one of these two categories, you have made an excellent decision on purchasing this book.

Python programming language has occupied the top spot for the last four years among the most wanted programming languages as per stackoverflow.com developer surveys. This fact shows the current industry trends where more and more developers are shifting toward Python and for the right reasons.

With the rise of data science and high-performance computing hardware, the interest in learning Python programming has been revitalized. Furthermore, Python is an extremely easy-to-learn and thoroughly versatile language that can be used for almost all types of programming tasks.

Thank you for your decision on purchasing this book. I can assure you that you will not regret your decision.

In this book, you will learn all these concepts. So, buckle up for a journey that may give you your career break!

## § Book Approach

The book follows a very simple approach. It is divided into 13 chapters, followed by three simple projects. The first 7 chapters of this book explain the environment set, software installation, and the core Python programming concepts such as Python syntax, data types and variables, conditional and decision statements, functions and methods, exception handling, and object-oriented programming. The last 6 chapters of the book are geared toward the explanation of some of the most useful Python libraries and utilities.

Each chapter explains the concepts theoretically, followed by practical examples. Each chapter also contains exercises that students can use to evaluate their understanding of the concepts explained in the chapter. The Python notebook for each chapter is provided in the *Resources Folder* that accompanies this book. It is advised that instead of copying the code from the book, you write the code yourself, and in case of an error, you match your code with the corresponding Python notebook, find and then correct the error. The datasets used in this book are either downloaded at runtime or are available in the *Resources* folder. Do not try to copy and paste the code from the PDF notebook, as you might face an indentation issue. If you have to copy some code, copy it from the Python Notebooks.

## § Who Is This Book For?

The book is aimed ideally at absolute beginners to Python programming in specific and programming in general. If you are a beginner-level programmer, you can use this book as a first introduction to programming. If you are already familiar with another programming language and now looking for an introductory resource to learn Python language, this book serves the purpose for you, too. Finally, if you are an experienced Python programmer, you can also use this book for general reference to perform common tasks in Python, data science, and machine learning.

Since this book is aimed at absolute beginners, the only prerequisites to efficiently using this book are the access to a computer with the internet and basic knowledge of linear algebra and calculus. All the codes and datasets have been provided. However, to download the data preparation libraries, you will need the internet.

## § How to Use This Book?

To get the best out of this book, I would suggest that you read the chapters of this book in order since the concepts taught in subsequent chapters are based on the concepts taught in previous chapters. In each chapter, try to first understand the usage of a specific Python concept and then try to execute the example code. I would again stress that rather than copying and pasting code, try to write codes yourself, and in case of any error, you can match your code with the source code provided in the book as well as in the Python notebooks in the *Resources* folder.

Finally, try to answer the questions asked in the exercises at the end of each chapter. The solutions to the exercises have been given at the end of the Book.

To facilitate the reading process, occasionally, the book presents three types of box-tags in different colors: **Requirements**, **Further Readings**, and **Hands-on Time**. Examples of these boxes are shown below.

**Requirements**

This box lists all requirements needed to be done before proceeding to the next topic. Generally, it works as a checklist to see if everything is ready before a tutorial.

**Further Readings**

Here, you will be pointed to some external reference or source that will serve as additional content about the specific **Topic** being studied. In general, it consists of packages, documentations, and cheat sheets.

**Hands-on Time**

Here, you will be pointed to an external file to train and test all the knowledge acquired about a **Tool** that has been studied. Generally, these files are Jupyter notebooks (.ipynb), Python (.py) files, or documents (.pdf).

The box-tag **Requirements** lists the steps required by the reader after reading one or more topics. **Further Readings** provides relevant references for specific topics to get to know the additional content of the topics. **Hands-on Time** points to practical tools to start working on the specified topics. Follow the instructions given in the box-tags to get a better understanding of the topics presented in this book.

# About the Author

M. Usman Malik holds a Ph.D. in Computer Science from Normandy University, France, with Artificial Intelligence and Machine Learning being his main areas of research. Muhammad Usman Malik has over 5 years of industry experience in Data Science and has worked with both private and public sector organizations. In his free time, he likes to listen to music and play snooker. You can follow his Twitter handle: @usman_malikk.

# 1

# Introduction

This chapter provides a very brief introduction to the Python programming language. You will study the history of the Python programming language, along with its unique characteristics and uses. You will also see some of the most common IDEs for Python development. The process of environment setup is also explained in the chapter. Finally, you will see how to run your first Python program. The chapter concludes with information about Python syntax.

## 1.1. History of Python

Though Python has recently risen to fame, owing largely to the boom in the domain of data science and artificial intelligence, it was first conceived in the early 1980s.

The work on the development of the Python programming language was started by Guido Van Rossum in 1989. Guido Van Rossum was looking forward to an interesting project that could keep him busy during the Christmas break and started developing a high-level language that would succeed the ABC programming language. The inspiration for the name came from BBC's TV Show –*Monty Python's Flying Circus*, as he was a big fan of the TV show. Python was finally released in 1991.

When the language was released, it had many unique characteristics. Python gained immediate popularity as it was compact compared to Java, C++, and C and required fewer lines of code to achieve the same task. It was easier to learn and update Python owing to the flexibility of syntax. Currently, Python 3.9.2 is the latest version of the Python programming language.

## 1.2. Uses of Python

Owing to its compactness and flexibility, tech giants such as Google, Dropbox, Quora, Facebook, Mozilla, Hewlett-Packard, Microsoft, Qualcomm, IBM, and Cisco have incorporated Python in their products in one way or the other.

Python is a very flexible language and can be used to develop a variety of application types, some of which are enlisted below:

1. **Desktop Development**

   Python is widely used for developing desktop-based applications. Python contains a variety of libraries, such as PyQt, PyGUI, Kivy, and WxPython, that can be used to develop beautiful GUI-based desktop applications.

2. **Web Development**

   A programming language is of no use if you cannot develop web applications with it. A python developer has the luxury of gaining access to various libraries like HTTPS, FTP, and SSL. Furthermore, various development frameworks such as Django and flask exist, which you can use to quickly develop a basic platform for your web applications.

3. **Data Science and Machine Learning**

   The term *data is the new oil* is no more a cliché. With the advent of big data and high-performance computing hardware, several Python libraries such as Scikit-learn, Numpy, Pandas, Matplotlib, TensorFlow, etc., have been developed. These libraries can be used to perform various data science related tasks, such as data visualization and manipulation, classification, regression, clustering via machine learning, and deep learning techniques.

4. **Game Development**

   You can use Python for the development of basic and advanced mobile and desktop games as well. You can use Python libraries like PySoy, which is a 3D game engine supporting Python 3. Popular games like Civilization IV, World of tanks, Disney's Toontown, and Battlefield 2 have been built using Python.

5. **Operating System Development**

   Python and C languages are often used in conjunction to develop operating systems. Python is compact and flexible, while the C language is extremely fast. The combination of Python and C has resulted in some of the greatest operating systems, e.g., Linux's Ubuntu and Fedora.

## 1.3. Commonly used Python IDEs

You can write a Python program with a text editor as simple as the notepad. However, several advanced tools have been developed that offer functionalities that can expedite Python development. Such tools are called Integrated Development Environments. Some of the most commonly used Python IDEs are enlisted below:

1. **Atom**

   Developed by Github, Atom is an extremely lightweight IDE that supports development in multiple languages, including Python. Atom supports syntax highlighting, IntelliSense, and easy installation of various Python packages. Atom is open source and free of cost.

2. **Visual Studio Code**

   Visual Studio Code is one of the most advanced programming IDE. With features like static and dynamic debugging, syntax highlighting, error highlighting, and version control, Visual Studio Code is one of the most widely used IDE not only for Python but also for other programming languages, as well. The community version of visual studio code is also freely downloadable.

3. **PyCharm**

   PyCharm, as the name suggests, helps you develop Python applications like a charm. Developed by JetBrains, PyCharm comes with some of the most premium features for Python development. Version control system, IntelliSense, code refactoring, code debugging and inspection, error-highlighting, and fixing are some of the most common features of PyCharm. PyCharm's trial version is free for one month. You have to buy the premium version after that.

4. **Spyder**

   Spyder is an open-source IDE for scientific computing and can also be used for Python development. Like all the other advanced Python editors, Spyder supports static and dynamic debugging, syntax highlighting, error highlighting, and version control. The easiest way to get up and running with Spyder is by installing Anaconda distribution. Anaconda is a popular distribution for data science and machine learning.

5. **Jupyter Notebook**

   The official website of the Jupyter Notebook defines Jupyter as "an open-source web application that allows you to create and share documents that contain live code, equations, visualizations, and narrative text." Jupyter notebook is an excellent tool for Python development if you are new to Python. With Jupyter notebook, you can write and execute your Python programs in small chunks using Jupyter cells. Jupyter can also be downloaded as a part of Anaconda distribution.

The choice of IDE depends totally on your personal preferences. In this book, you will be downloading the Anaconda distribution of Python, which will also download Spyder and Jupyter IDEs for you. The Python scripts in this book have been written and tested with the Jupyter IDE.

## 1.4. Environment Setup

### 1.4.1. Windows Setup

The time has come to install Python on Windows using an IDE. We will use Anaconda throughout this book, right from installing Python to writing multi-threaded codes in the coming lectures. Now, let us get going with the installation.

This section explains how you can download and install Anaconda on Windows.

Follow these steps to download and install Anaconda.

1. Open the following URL in your browser.

   https://www.anaconda.com/products/individual

2. The browser will take you to the following webpage. Depending upon your OS, select the 64-bit or 32-bit Graphical Installer file for Windows. Based on the speed of your internet, the file will download within 2–3 minutes.

3. Run the executable file after the download is complete. You will most likely find the download file in your download folder. The installation wizard will open when you run the file, as shown in the following figure. Click the *Next* button.

4. Now click *I Agree* on the License Agreement dialog, as shown in the following screenshot.

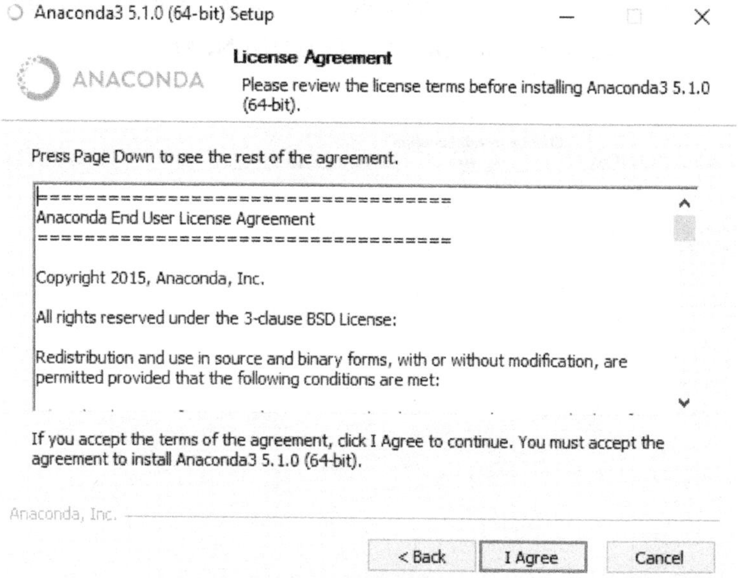


5. Check the *Just Me* radio button from the Select Installation Type dialogue box. Click the **Next** button to continue.

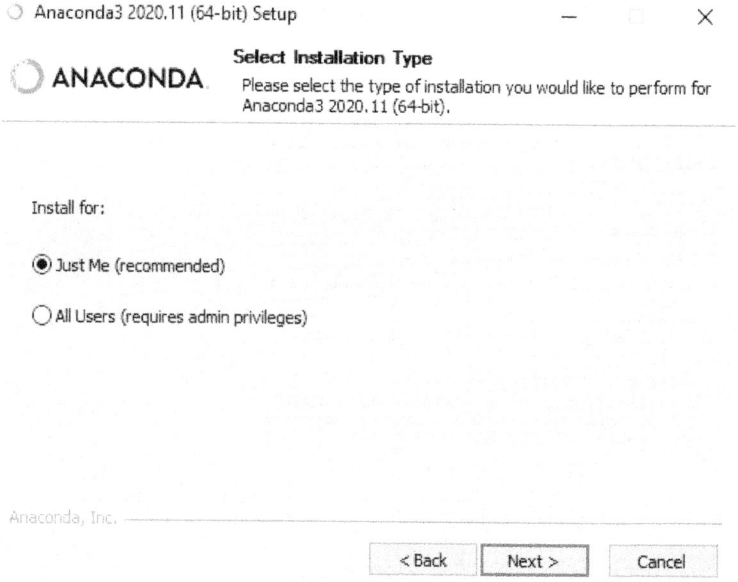

6. Now, the Choose Install Location dialog will be displayed. Change the directory if you want, but the default is preferred. The installation folder should at least have 3 GB of free space for Anaconda. Click the **Next** button.

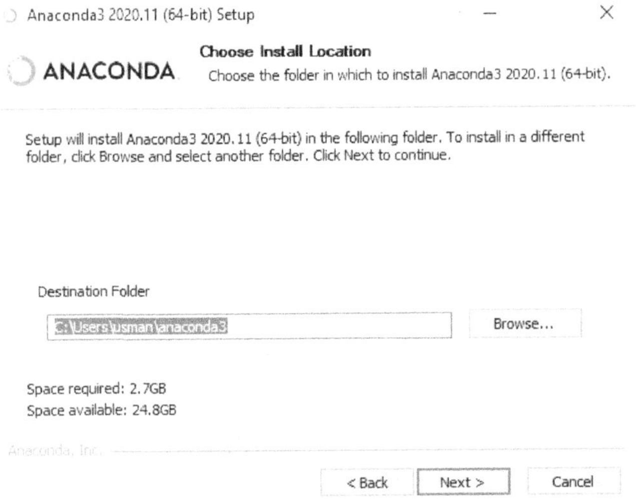


7. Go for the second option, Register Anaconda as my default Python 3.8, in the Advanced Installation Options dialogue box. Click the **Install** button to start the installation, which can take some time to complete.

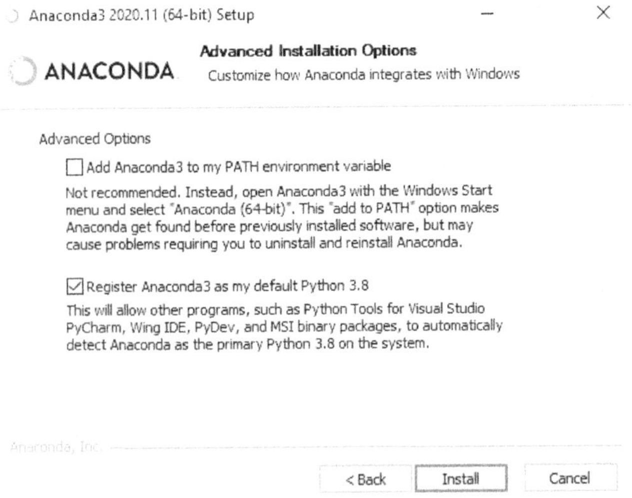

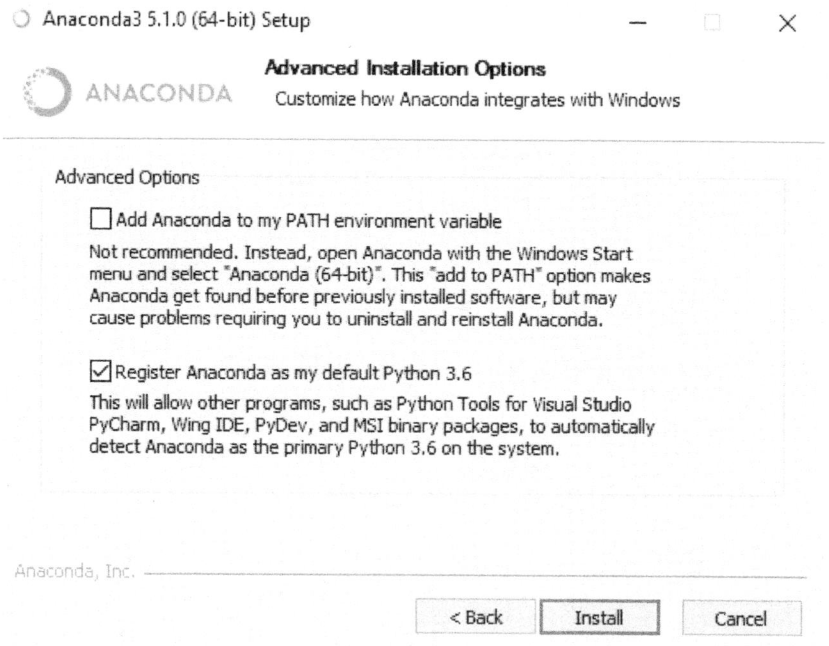


8. Click **Next** once the installation is complete.

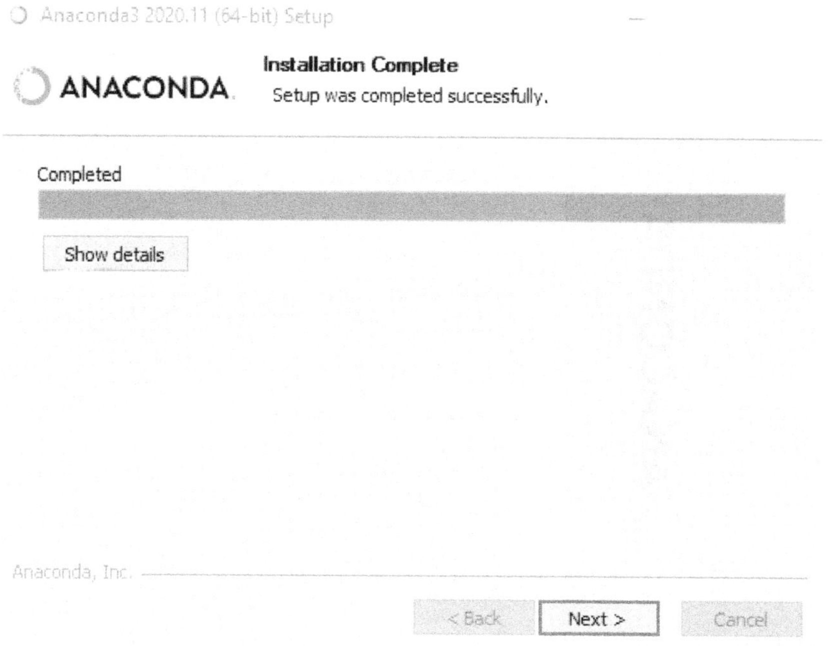

9. Click **Skip** on the Microsoft Visual Studio Code Installation dialog box.

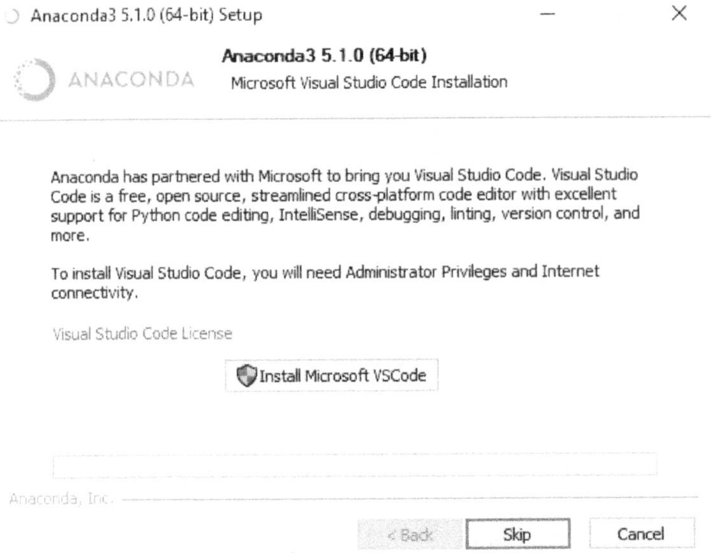


10. You have successfully installed Anaconda on your Windows. Excellent job. The next step is to uncheck both checkboxes on the dialog box. Now, click on the **Finish** button.

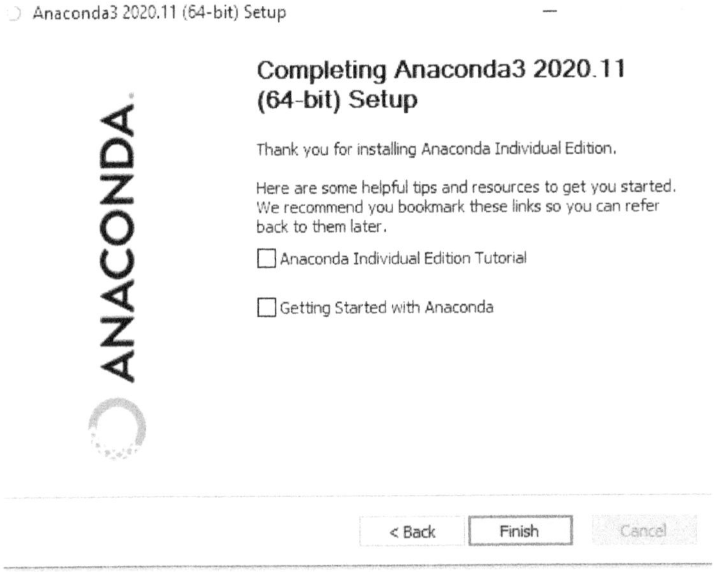

## 1.4.2. Mac Setup

Anaconda's installation process is almost the same for Mac. It may differ graphically, but you will follow the same steps you followed for Windows. The only difference is that you have to download the executable file, which is compatible with Mac operating system.

This section explains how you can download and install Anaconda on Mac.

Follow these steps to download and install Anaconda.

1. Open the following URL in your browser.

   https://www.anaconda.com/products/individual

2. The browser will take you to the following webpage. Depending upon your OS, select the 64-bit or 32-bit Graphical Installer file for macOS. Based on the speed of your internet, the file will download within 2-3 minutes.

3. Run the executable file after the download is complete. You will most likely find the download file in your download folder. The name of the file should be similar to "Anaconda3-5.1.0-Windows-x86_64." The installation wizard will open when you run the file, as shown in the following figure. Click the **Continue** button.

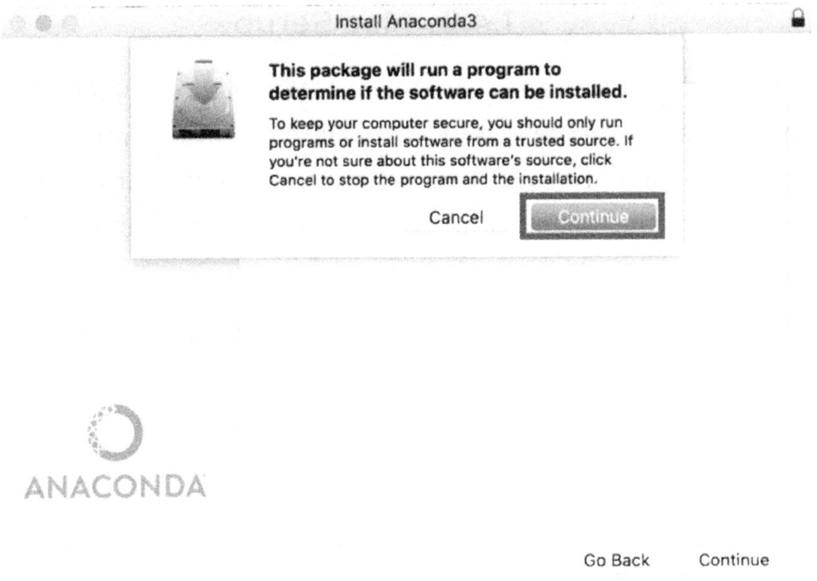


4. Now click **Continue** on the "Welcome to Anaconda 3 Installer" window, as shown in the following screenshot.

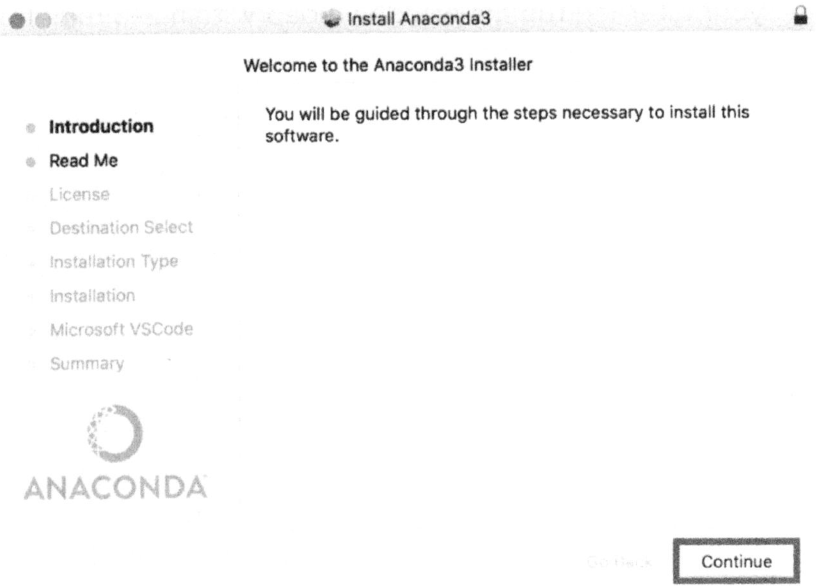

5. The *Important Information* dialog will pop up. Simply, click **Continue** to go with the default version that is Anaconda 3.

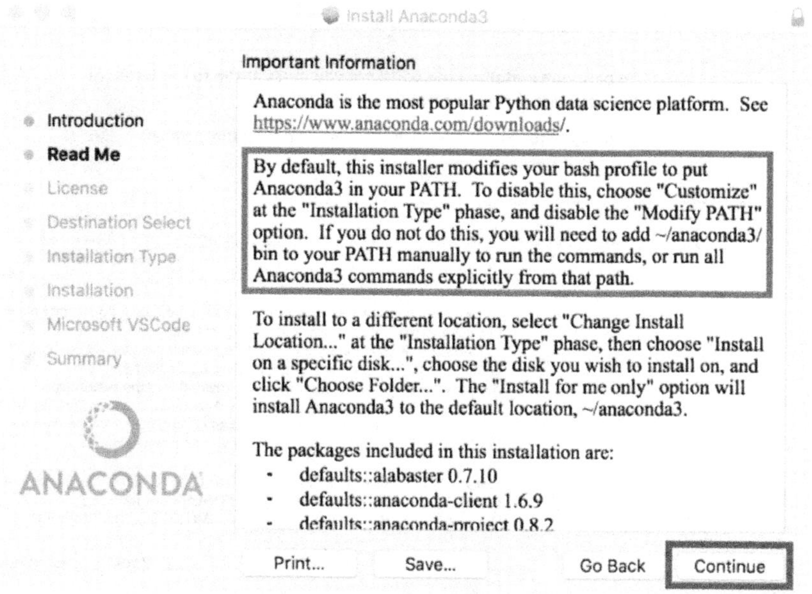


6. Click *Continue* on the Software License Agreement Dialog.

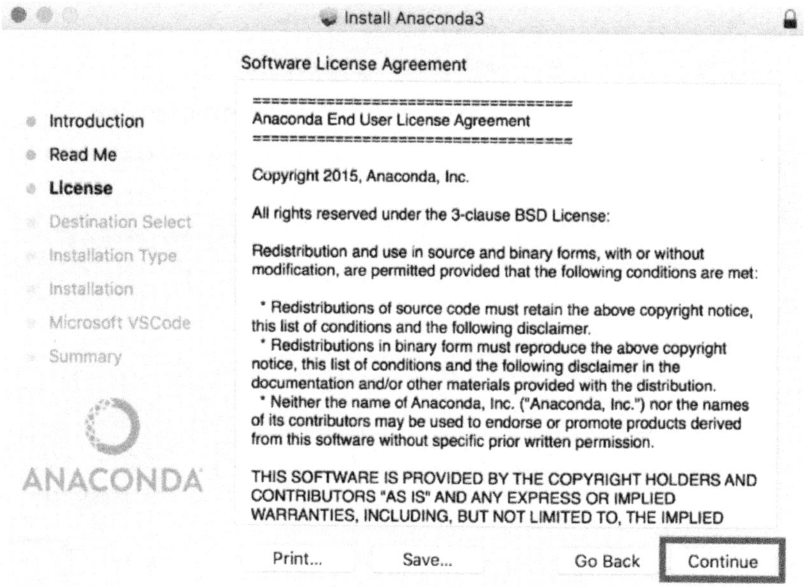

7. It is mandatory to read the license agreement and click the **Agree** button before you can click the **Continue** button again.

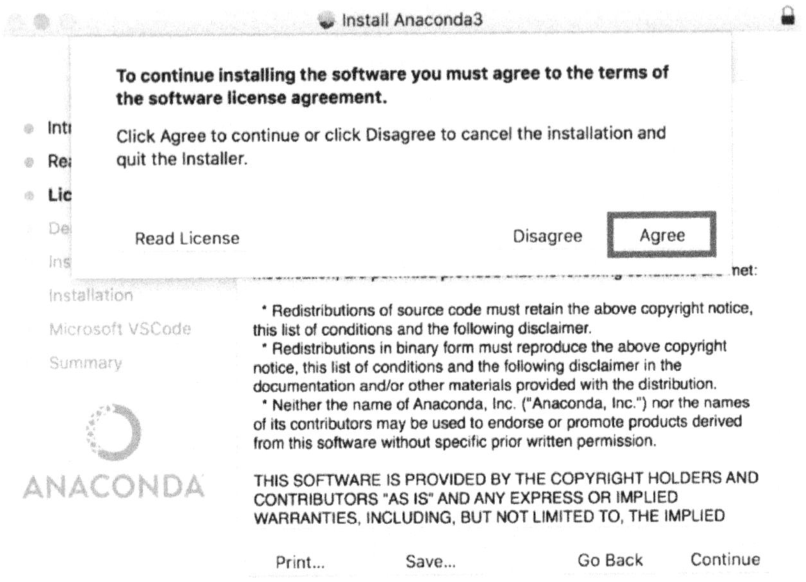


8. Simply click **Install** on the next window that appears.

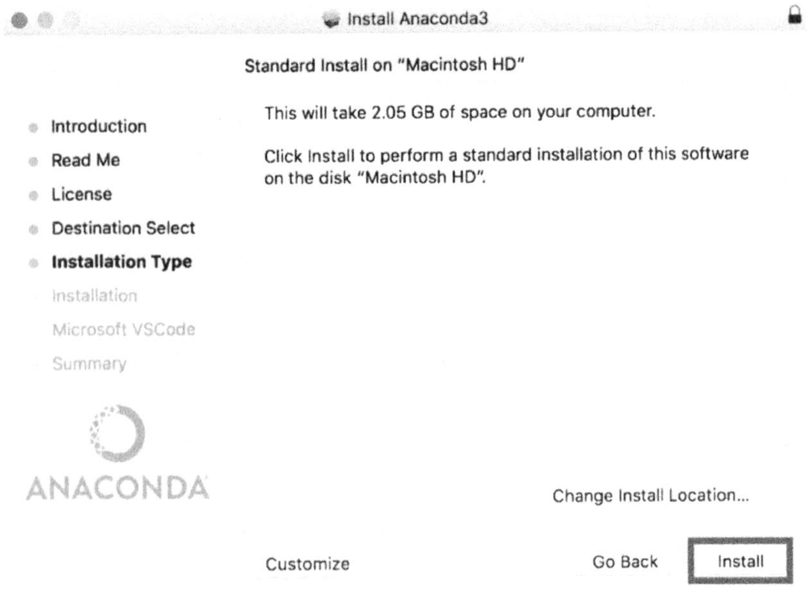

The system will prompt you to give your password. Use the same password you use to log in to your Mac computer. Now, click on *Install Software*.

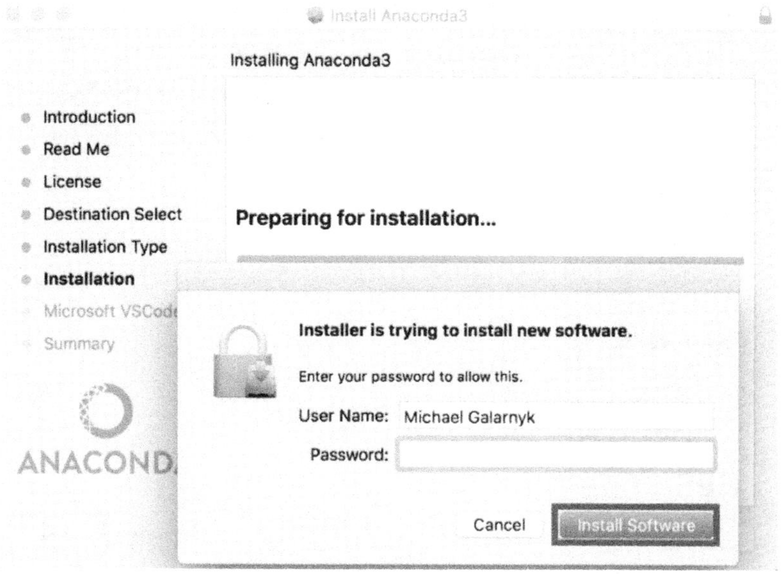


9. Click **Continue** on the next window. You also have the option to install Microsoft VSCode at this point.

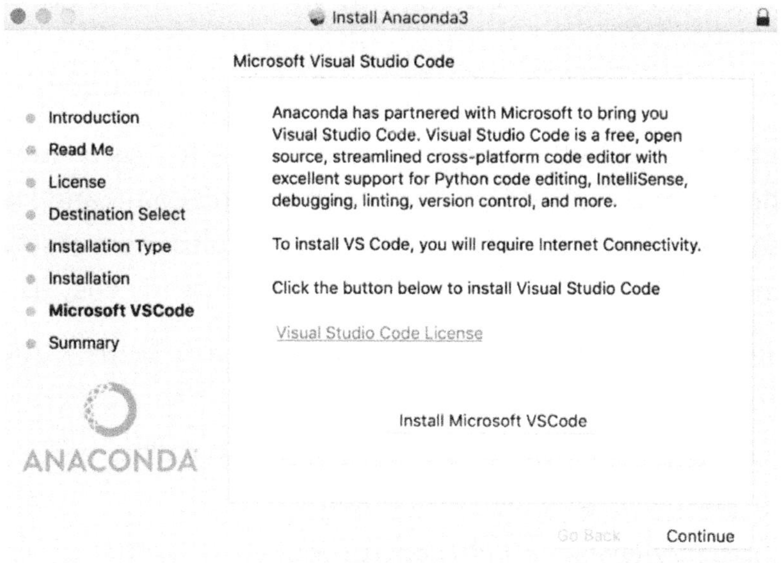

The next screen will display the message that the installation has been completed successfully. Click on the *Close* button to close the installer.

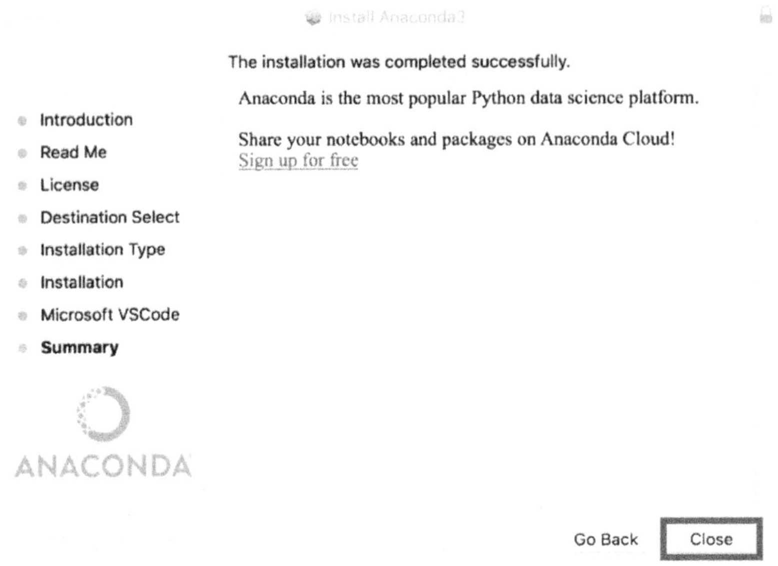


There you have it. You have successfully installed Anaconda on your Mac computer. Now, you can write Python code in Jupyter and Spyder the same way you wrote it in Windows.

### 1.4.3. Linux Setup

We have used Python's graphical installers for installation on Windows and Mac. However, we will use the command line to install Python on Ubuntu or Linux. Linux is also more resource-friendly, and installation of software is particularly easy as well.

Follow these steps to install Anaconda on Linux (Ubuntu distribution).

1. Go to the following link to copy the installer bash script from the latest available version.

   https://www.anaconda.com/products/individual

2. The second step is to download the installer bash script. Log into your Linux computer and open your terminal. Now, go to /temp directory and download the bash you downloaded from Anaconda's home page using curl.

```
$ cd / tmp

$ curl -o https://repo.anaconda.com.archive/Anaconda3-
    5.2.0-Linux-x86_64.sh
```

3. You should also use the cryptographic hash verification through SHA-256 checksum to verify the integrity of the installer.

```
$ sha256sum Anaconda3-5.2.0-Linux-x86_64.sh
```

You will get the following output.

```
09f53738b0cd3bb96f5b1bac488e5528df9906be2480fe61df40e0e0d19e3d48
Anaconda3-5.2.0-Linux-x86_64.sh
```

4. The fourth step is to run the Anaconda Script, as shown in the following figure.

```
$ bash Anaconda3-5.2.0-Linux-x86_64.sh
```

The command line will produce the following output. You will be asked to review the license agreement. Keep on pressing *Enter* until you reach the end.

```
Output

Welcome to Anaconda3 5.2.0

In order to continue the installation process, please
review the license agreement.
Please, press Enter to continue.
>>>
...
Do you approve the license terms? [yes|No]
```

Type *Yes* when you get to the bottom of the License Agreement.

5. The installer will ask you to choose the installation location after you agree to the license agreement. Simply press *Enter* to choose the default location. You can also specify a different location if you want.

```
Output

Anaconda3 will now be installed on this location:
/home/tola/anaconda3

- Press ENTER to confirm the location
- Press CTRL-C to abort the installation
- Or specify a different location below

[/home/tola/anaconda3] >>>
```

The installation will proceed once you press *Enter*. Once again, you have to be patient as the installation process takes some time to complete.

6. You will receive the following result when the installation is complete. If you wish to use the conda command, type *Yes*.

```
Output
...
Installation finished.
Do you wish the installer to prepend Anaconda3 install
location to path in your /home/tola/.bashrc? [yes|no]
[no]>>>
```

At this point, you will also have the option to download the Visual Studio Code. Type *yes* or *no* to install or decline, respectively.

7. Use the following command to activate your brand-new installation of Anaconda3.

```
$ source `/.bashrc
```

8. You can also test the installation using the conda command.

```
$ conda list
```

Congratulations. You have successfully installed Anaconda on your Linux system.

### 1.4.4. Using Google Colab Cloud Environment

In addition to local Python environments such as Anaconda, you can run deep learning applications on Google Colab as well, which is Google's platform for deep learning with GPU support. All the codes in this book have been run using Google Colab. Therefore, I would suggest that you use Google Colab too.

To run deep learning applications via Google Colab, all you need is a Google/Gmail account. Once you have a Google/Gmail account, you can simply go to:

https://colab.research.google.com/

Next, click on File -> New notebook, as shown in the following screenshot.

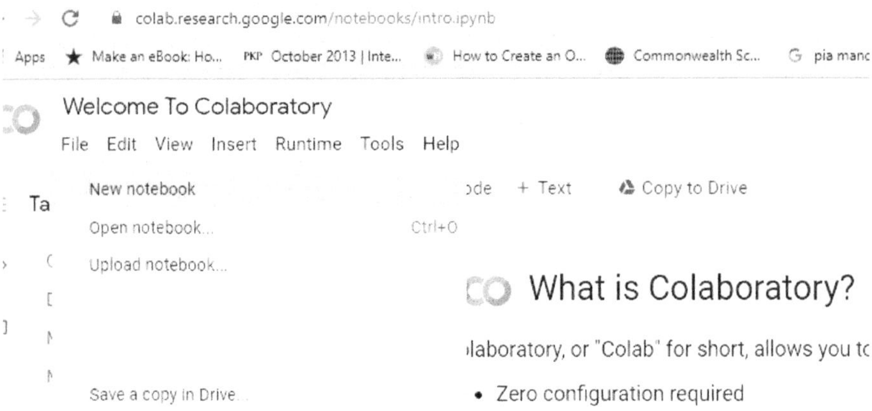


Next, to run your code using GPU, from the top menu, select Runtime -> Change runtime type, as shown in the following screenshot:

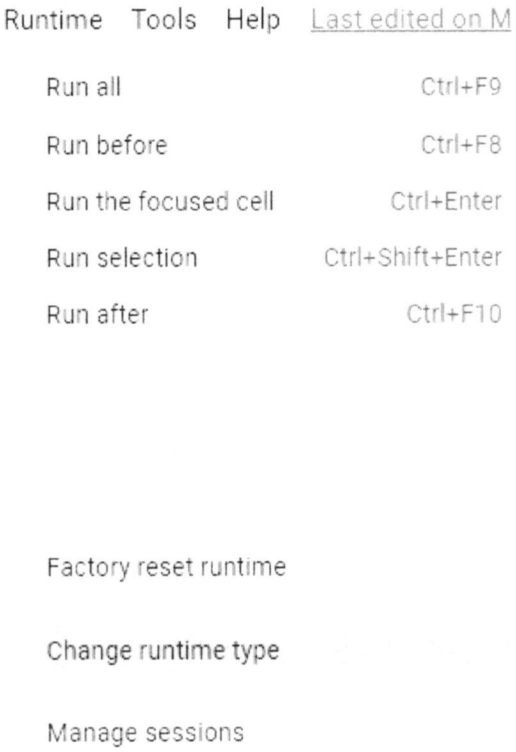

You should see the following window. Here, from the dropdown list, select GPU and click the **Save** button.

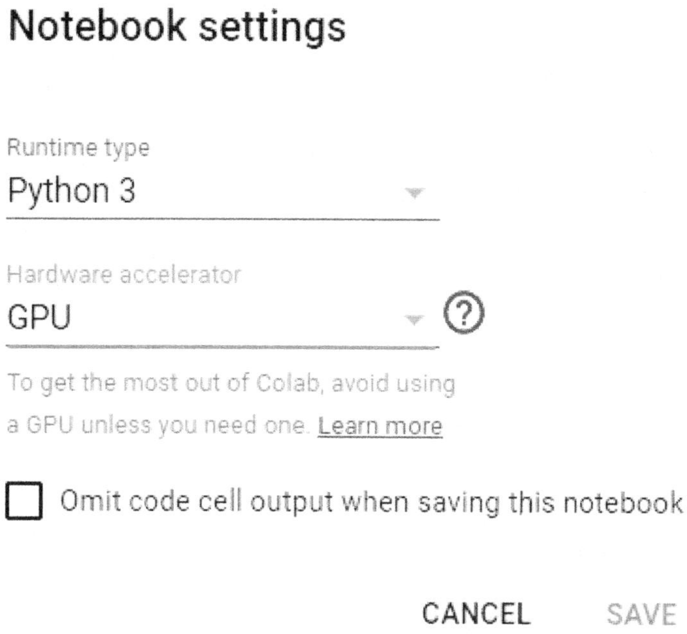


To make sure you are running the latest version of TensorFlow, execute the following script in the Google Colab notebook cell. The following script will update your TensorFlow version.

```
pip install --upgrade tensorflow
```

To check if you are really running TensorFlow version > 2.0, execute the following script.

```
import tensorflow as tf
print(tf.__version__)
```

With Google Cloud, you can import the datasets from your Google drive. Execute the following script. And click on the link that appears, as shown below:

```
from google.colab import drive
drive.mount('/gdrive')
```

```
Go to this URL in a browser: https://accounts.google.com/o/oauth2/auth

Enter your authorization code:
```

You will be prompted to allow Google Colab to access your Google drive. Click *Allow* button as shown below:

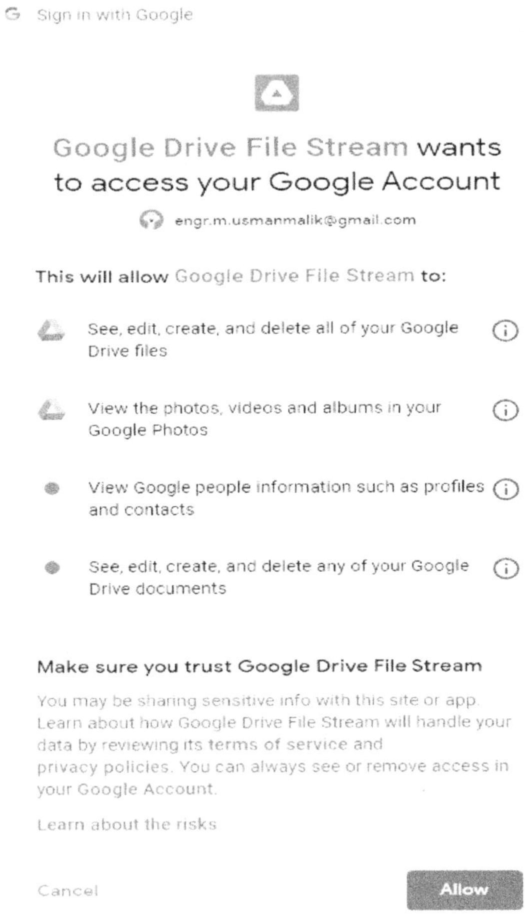


You will see a link appear, as shown in the following image (The link has been blinded here).

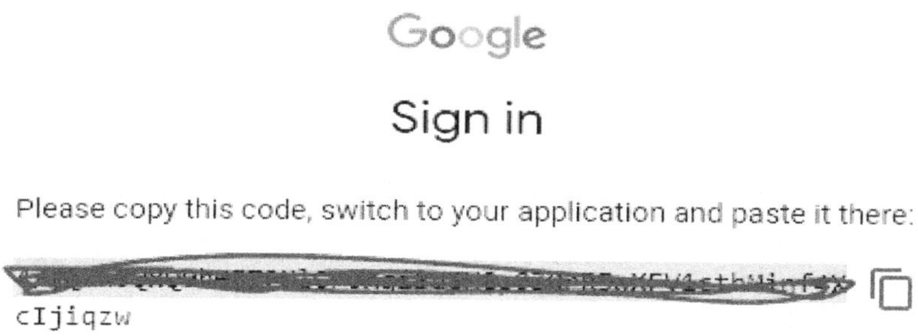


Copy the link and paste it in the empty field in the Google Colab cell, as shown below:

```
from google.colab import drive
drive.mount('/gdrive')

Go to this URL in a browser: https://accounts.google.com/o/oauth2/auth

Enter your authorization code:
```

This way, you can import datasets from your Google drive to your Google Colab environment.

## 1.5. Writing Your First Program

You have already installed Python on your computer and established a unique environment in the form of Anaconda. Now, it is time to write your first program, that is *Hello World!*

To write a program in Anaconda, you have to launch Anaconda Navigator. Search "Anaconda Navigator" in your Windows Search Box. Now, click on the Anaconda Navigator application icon, as shown in the following figure.

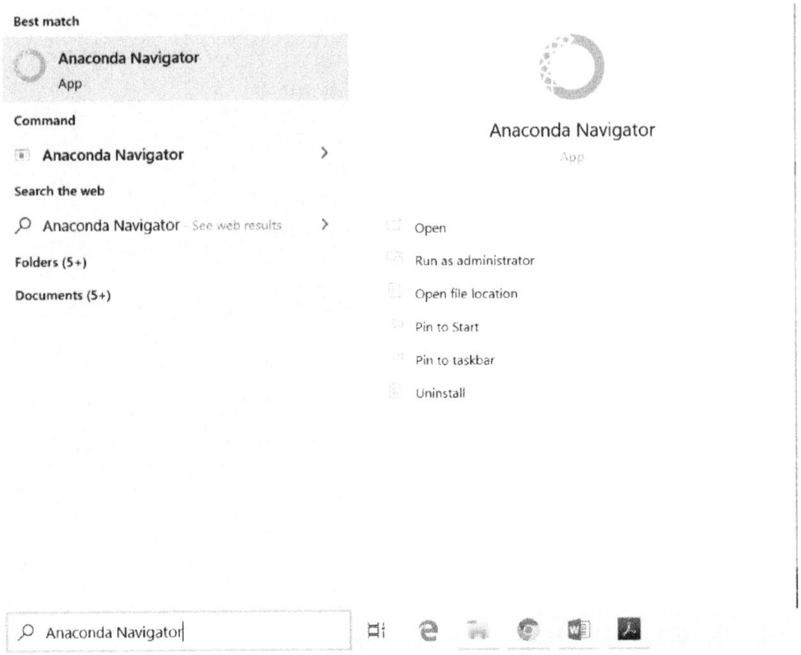


Once you click on the application, Anaconda's Dashboard will open. The Dashboard offers you a myriad of tools to write your code. We will use the *Jupyter Notebook*, the most popular of these tools, to write and explain the code throughout this book.

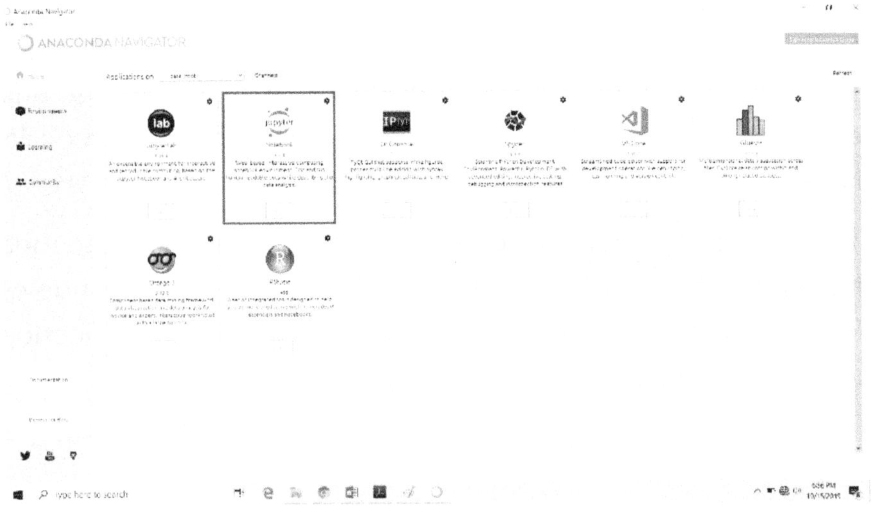

The Jupyter Notebook is available in the second position from the top of the dashboard. You can use Jupyter Notebook even if you don't have access to the internet as it runs right in your default browser. Another method to open Jupyter Notebook is to type Jupyter Notebook in the Window's search bar. Subsequently, click on the Jupyter Notebook application. The application will open in the new tab of your browser.

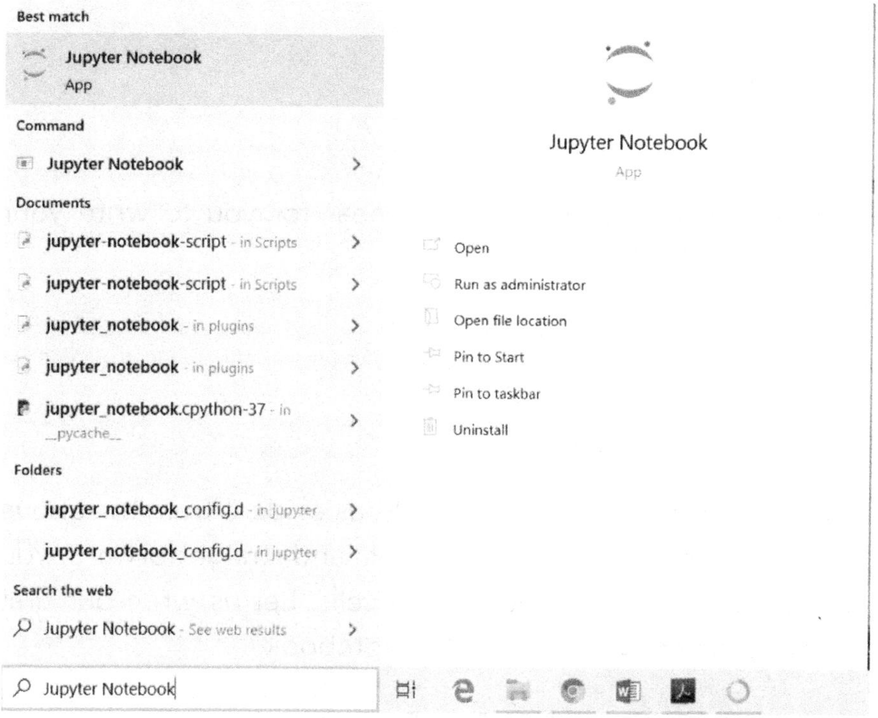


The top right corner of Jupyter Notebook's own dashboard houses a *New* button, which you have to click to open a new document. A dropdown containing several options will appear. Click on *Python 3*.

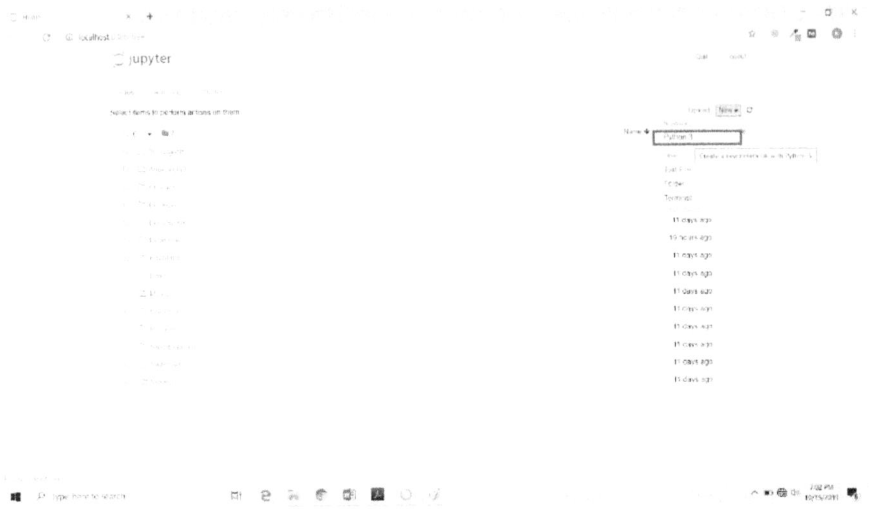


A new Jupyter Notebook will appear for you to write your programs. It looks as follows.

Jupyter Notebook consists of cells, as evident from the above image, making its layout very simple and straightforward. You will write your code inside these cells. Let us write our first ever Python program in Jupyter Notebook.

### 1.3.1. Writing Your First Program

```
In [1]: print("Welcome to Data Visualization with Python")

        Welcome to Data Visualization with Python
```

The above script prints a string value in the output using the **print()** method. The **print()** method is used to print on the console any string passed to it. If you see the following output, you have successfully run your first Python program.

**Output:**

```
Welcome to Data Visualization with Python
```

Let's now explore some of the other important Python concepts starting with Variables and Data Types.

**Requirements – Anaconda, Jupyter, and Matplotlib**

- All the scripts in this book have been executed via Jupyter Notebook. Therefore, you should have Jupyter Notebook installed. The other option is to use Google Colab's Jupyter Notebook.

# 1.6. Python Syntax

Syntax of a language is a set of rules that the developer or the person writing the code must follow for the successful execution of code. Just like natural languages such as English have grammar and spelling rules, programming languages have their own rules.

In this article, we will see the syntax of the Python programming language.

## § Keywords

Every programming language has a specific set of words that perform specific functions and cannot be used as a variable or identifier. Python has the following set of keywords:

| False | class | finally | is | return |
|---|---|---|---|---|
| None | continue | for | lambda | try |
| True | def | from | nonlocal | while |
| and | del | global | not | with |
| as | elif | if | or | yield |
| assert | else | import | pass | |
| break | except | in | raise | |

For instance, the keyword *class* is used to create a new class in Python. (We will see classes in detail in a later chapter.) Furthermore, the *if* keyword creates an *if* condition. If you try to use any of these keywords as variables, you will see errors.

## § Python Statements

Statements in Python are the smallest units of executable code. When you assign a value to an identifier, you basically write a statement. For example, age = 10 is a Python statement. When Python executes this statement, it assigns a value of 10 to the age identifier.

```
age =10
print(age)
```

The script above has two statements. The first statement assigns a value of 10 to the age identifier. The second statement prints the age identifier.

If your statements are too long, you can span them by enclosing them in parenthesis, braces, or brackets as shown below:

```
message =("This is a message"
"it spans multiple lines")

print(message)
```

**Output:**

```
This is a message it spans multiple lines
```

Another way to write a statement on multiple lines is by adding a backslash (\) at the end of the first line. Look at the following script:

```
message ="This is a message" \
"it spans multiple lines"

print(message)
```

The output is the same as that of the previous script.

## § Indentation

Indentation is one of those features that distinguish Python from other advanced programming languages, such as C++, Java, and C#. In the other programming languages, normally, braces ({) are used to define a block of code.

Indentation is used to define a new block of code in Python. A block of code in Python is a set of Python statements that execute together. You will see blocks in action when you study loops and conditional statements.

To define a new block, you have to indent the Python code, one tab (or 4 spaces) from the left.

```
age =8
if age <10:
print("Age is less than 10")
print("You do not qualify")
else:
print("Age is greater than or equal to 10")
print("You do qualify")
```

**Output:**

```
Age is less than 10
You do not qualify
```

In the above code, we define an identifier **age** with a value of 8. We then use the *if* statement and check if age is less than or not. If the age is less than 10, then the first block of code executes, which prints two statements on the console. You can see that code blocks have been indented.

## § Comments

Comments are used to add notes to a program. Comments do not execute, and you don't have to declare them in the form of statements. Comments are used to explain the code so that if you take a look at the code after a long time, you understand what you did.

Comments can be of two types: Single line comments and double-line comments. To add single line comments, you simply have to add #, as shown below:

```
# The following statement adds two numbers

num =10+20# the result is 30
```

To add multi-line comments, you just need to add a # at the start of every line, as shown below:

```
#This is comment 1
#This is comment 2
#This is comment 3
```

Enough of the theory! From the next chapter, you will study what are Python Variables and Data Types and how to declare and use variables of different types in Python.

# 2

# Python Variables and Data Types

In this chapter, you will study Python variables, what are the different data types that you can work with within Python. What are the different functions that you can perform on different data types? So let's begin without any further ado.

## 2.1. Python Variables

A software application fundamentally consists of two parts: logic and data. The application logic manipulates application data.

The logic is implemented via various programming constructs such as conditional statements, iteration statements, exceptional handling, etc., which you will study in the upcoming chapters.

The application data can be stored on a hard disk or system memory. Hard disks, flat files, and databases are normally used to store application data. When the application is run, data is loaded from the hard drive or ROM and is loaded into in-memory variables. Variables store in-memory data.

## § What Are Variables?

In the literal sense, a variable is nothing but a chunk of named memory location which stores some data. Assigning a value to the variable refers to storing some data in a memory location with a specific name. The name of the memory location is also called the variable name.

To store data in a variable, the assignment operator = is used. The value to the left side of the assignment operator is the variable name or variable identifier. The value to the right side of the operator is the value that is being stored in the variable.

Look at the following script. Here, you initialize four variables of types string, integer, float, and Boolean. It is important to mention that you do not need to specify the data type with the variable name. The Python interpreter interprets the data type for the variable at runtime, depending upon the value being stored, and allocates memory size accordingly.

**Script 1:**

```
Name   ="James"# A string variable
Age    =15# An integer variable
Weight =70.5# A floating type variable
Married  =True# A boolean Variable
```

You can check the data type of a variable by passing the variable to the builtin**type()** function, as shown below:

**Script 2:**

```
print(type(Name))
print(type(Age))
print(type(Weight))
print(type(Married))
```

**Output:**

```
<class 'str'>
<class 'int'>
<class 'float'>
<class 'bool'>
```

In addition to a single assignment, you can also assign one value to multiple variables. To do so, you will have to chain multiple variable names using an assignment operator, as shown in the following script:

**Script 3:**

```
Name = Weight = Married =True

print(Name)
print(Weight)
print(Married)
```

The output shows that all three variables, i.e., Name, Weight, and Married contain a Boolean True as their values.

**Output:**

```
True
True
True
```

## 2.2. Python Data Types

Python data types can be broadly divided into the following main categories:

1. Numeric Types
2. String Types
3. Boolean Types
4. Lists

5. Tuples
6. Dictionaries

### 2.2.1. Numeric Types

Python numeric types store numeric data such as integers, floats, complex numbers, binary numbers, etc.

#### § Integers

To create an integer type variable, simply store an integer value in any variable name, as shown below. If you check the type of the variable, you will see that it outputs <class 'int'>. When you create an integer, you create an object of the integer class.

**Script 4:**

```
int_num=25
print(type(int_num))
```

**Output:**

```
<class 'int'>
```

You can check all the methods and attributes associated with an object using the **dir()**method, as shown below. You will study methods and attributes in detail in a later chapter. For now, just remember that methods perform some functionality while attributes store some data related to an object.

**Script 5:**

```
dir(int_num)
```

**Output:**

```
['__abs__',
 '__add__',
 '__and__',
 '__bool__',
 '__ceil__',
 '__class__',
 '__delattr__',
 '__dir__',
 '__divmod__',
 '__doc__',
 '__eq__',
 '__float__',
 '__floor__',
 '__floordiv__',
 '__format__',
 '__ge__',
 '__getattribute__',
 '__getnewargs__',
 '__gt__',
 '__hash__',
 '__index__',
 '__init__',
 '__init_subclass__',
 '__int__',
 '__invert__',
 '__le__',
 '__lshift__',
 '__lt__',
 '__mod__',
 '__mul__',
 '__ne__',
 '__neg__',
 '__new__',
 '__or__',
 '__pos__',
 '__pow__',
 '__radd__',
 '__rand__',
```

```
'__rdivmod__',
'__reduce__',
'__reduce_ex__',
'__repr__',
'__rfloordiv__',
'__rlshift__',
'__rmod__',
'__rmul__',
'__ror__',
'__round__',
'__rpow__',
'__rrshift__',
'__rshift__',
'__rsub__',
'__rtruediv__',
'__rxor__',
'__setattr__',
'__sizeof__',
'__str__',
'__sub__',
'__subclasshook__',
'__truediv__',
'__trunc__',
'__xor__',
'as_integer_ratio',
'bit_length',
'conjugate',
'denominator',
'from_bytes',
'imag',
'numerator',
'real',
'to_bytes']
```

## § Floats

To create a floating type variable, you just have to declare a number with decimals, as shown below:

**Script 6:**

```
flt_num=2.6554
print(type(flt_num))
```

**Output:**

```
<class 'float'>
```

You can also create a floating variable using the "e" value to define exponents.

**Script 7:**

```
flt_num=2.6554e3
print(flt_num)
print(type(flt_num))
```

**Output:**

```
2655.4
<class 'float'>
```

## § Complex Numbers

Complex numbers are numbers that consist of a real number and an imaginary part. You can also create variables that store complex numbers in Python, as shown in the following script:

**Script 8:**

```
cmp_num=-.785+7J
print(type(cmp_num))
```

**Output:**

```
<class 'complex'>
```

## § Binary Numbers

Binary numbers store data in the form of 1s and 0s. You can define binary numbers in python by prefixing "0b" before a binary number. The binary numbers are converted into integers when you try to print them or check their type. Look at the following script for reference.

**Script 9:**

```
bin_num=0b11010000
print(bin_num)
print(type(bin_num))
```

**Output:**

```
208
<class 'int'>
```

## 2.2.2. Strings

Strings store textual data in Python, such as names, addresses, credit card numbers, and any text which contains letters. Python strings are treated as sequences of characters.

To create a python string, you simply have to wrap any text within single or double quotes. The following script creates a string literal and prints it on a console.

**Script 10:**

```
print("This is a string literal")
```

**Output:**

```
This is a string literal
```

You can also store a string in a variable. The following script stores a string in a variable and then prints the type of the string variable.

**Script 11:**

```
str_var="This is a variable inside a string"
print(str_var)
print(type(str_var))
```

**Output:**

```
This is a variable inside a string
<class 'str'>
```

## § Multi-line Strings

To create a string that spans multiple lines, you have to wrap a string in triple quotes, as shown in the following script:

**Script 12:**

```
str_mul="""Hell this string
spans on multiple lines
and this is the last line"""

print(str_mul)
```

**Output:**

```
Hell this string
spans on multiple lines
and this is the last line
```

## § Single and Double Quotes in Strings

You will often need to add single and double quotes within a string. To add a single-quoted text inside a string, try to wrap the overall string in double quotes. The following string contains a single-quoted string inside another string.

**Script 13:**

```
single_quote="This is a string 'single quoted' value"
print(single_quote)
```

**Output:**

```
This is a string 'single quoted' value
```

On the other hand, if you want to add double-quoted substring inside another string, wrap the overall string with single quotes, as shown in the following script.

**Script 14:**

```
double_quote='This is a string "double quoted" value'
print(double_quote)
```

**Output:**

```
This is a string "double quoted" value
```

## § String Concatenation

String concatenation refers to joining two strings.

Before string concatenation, let's see how you can access a single character within a string. As I said earlier, a string is a sequence of characters. The first character occurs at the $0^{th}$ index. Hence, if you want to access the second character, you can use the following syntax.

**Script 15:**

```
my_string="Hello this is a simple string"
my_string[1]
```

Since the second character in the string is "e," you can see the character "e" printed in the console output.

**Output:**

```
'e'
```

Also, you calculate the length, i.e., the number of characters in your string using the len() function, as shown below:

**Script 16:**

```
print(len(my_string))
```

**Output:**

```
29
```

Let's now see how you can add two strings. To do so, you can use the addition operator (+). The following script concatenates two strings, displays the concatenated string on the console, and then displays the length of the concatenated string.

**Script 17:**

```
string1 ="Hello how are you?"
string2 ="This is Mike!"
print(string1 + string2)
print(len(string1+string2))
```

**Output:**

```
Hello how are you? This is Mike!
32
```

### 2.2.3. Boolean Variables

Boolean variables, as the name suggests, can store either True or False values. In the following script, the Honda variable is by default False. It becomes true if the car variable contains the string "Honda."

**Script 18:**

```
car = "Honda"
isHonda = False

if car == "Honda":
   isHonda = True
else:
   isHonda = False

print(isHonda)
```

**Output:**

```
True
```

## 2.2.4. Lists

Lists in Python store a collection of items of the same or different types.

### § Creating Lists

To create a list, you have to add items inside a square bracket. The items should be separated by a comma. The following script creates a list of four strings containing color names.

**Script 19:**

```
colors =["Red","Green","Blue","Orange"]

print(colors)
print(type(colors))
```

**Output:**

```
['Red', 'Green', 'Blue', 'Orange']
<class 'list'>
```

You can also add items of different data types in a list, as shown in the following script:

**Script 20:**

```
mixed_list=[20,"Male","USA",True]
print(mixed_list)
```

**Output:**

```
[20, 'Male', 'USA', True]
```

## § Accessing List Elements

Python lists follow zero-based indexing where the first item is stored at the $0^{th}$ index, the second item is stored at the $1^{st}$ index, and so on.

To access a single list item, you need to specify its index inside a pair of square brackets that follow the list name. For instance, to get the item at the first index (second item) of the colors list, you can use the following syntax.

**Script 21:**

```
colors =["Red","Green","Blue","Orange"]
print(colors[1])
```

**Output:**

```
Green
```

You can also iterate through all the list items using a for loop. You will see for loops in chapter 4. For now, just keep in mind that you can also access sequentially iterate through list items.

**Script 22:**

```
for col in colors:
    print(col)
```

**Output:**

```
Red
Green
Blue
Orange
```

Since a Python list is a collection, you can find the number of items in a list using the len() function, as shown in the following script:

**Script 23:**

```
print(len(colors))
```

**Output:**

```
4
```

## § Adding Elements to a List

To add elements to a list, you can use the append() function. The following script appends a string to the colors list.

**Script 24:**

```
colors =["Red","Green","Blue","Orange"]
colors.append("Black")
print(colors)
```

In the output, you can see the newly added item.

**Output:**

```
['Red', 'Green', 'Blue', 'Orange', 'Black']
```

## § Updating a List

To update a list, you can simply access the list index for the item to be updated and assign a new item to that list index. In the following script, the second item in the colors list is replaced by the color "Yellow."

**Script 25:**

```
colors =["Red","Green","Blue","Orange"]
colors[1]="Yellow"
print(colors)
```

**Output:**

```
['Red', 'Yellow', 'Blue', 'Orange']
```

It is important to mention that you cannot access a list index that doesn't exist. For instance, in the colors list, there are 4 items. If you try to access an index for the 5th item, you will see an exception, as shown below:

**Script 26:**

```
colors[4]="Yellow"
print(colors)
```

**Output:**

```
---------------------------------------------------------------
IndexError                    Traceback (most recent call last)
<ipython-input-60-0ad7d039b30e> in <module>
----> 1colors[5]="Yellow"
      2 print(colors)

IndexError: list assignment index out of range
```

## § Deleting a List Item

To delete a list item, you have two options. You can either pass the item to the remove() function, as shown in the following script:

**Script 27:**

```
colors =["Red","Green","Blue","Orange"]
colors.remove("Green")
print(colors)
```

**Output:**

```
['Red', 'Blue', 'Orange']
```

The other option is to pass the list index to the pop() method of the list, as shown below:

**Script 28:**

```
colors =["Red","Green","Blue","Orange"]
colors.pop(2)
print(colors)
```

Since the item at index 2 was "Blue," it has been removed from the list.

**Output:**

```
['Red', 'Green', 'Orange']
```

## 2.2.5. Tuples

Tuples also store a collection of items, but tuples are immutable, which means that once created, you cannot modify, update, or delete items from a tuple.

### § Creating a Tuple

To create a tuple, you need to add items inside the round bracket or parenthesis. Like lists, the items in a tuple are separated by commas. The following script creates a tuple with 4 items.

**Script 29:**

```
my_tuple=("James",25,"Male",True)
print(my_tuple)
print(type(my_tuple))
```

**Output:**

```
('James', 25, 'Male', True)
<class 'tuple'>
```

## § Accessing Tuple Elements

Tuple items can also be accessed via indexes. For instance, the following script prints the second item of "my_tuple."

**Script 30:**

```
print(my_tuple[1])
```

**Output:**

```
25
```

You can also pass a negative index number to access items from the end of a tuple. For instance, to access the last item of a tuple, you can pass −1 as the index value.

**Script 31:**

```
print(my_tuple[-1])
```

**Output:**

```
True
```

**Note:** Negative indexing also works for lists.

Finally, you can also iterate through all the tuple items using a for loop, as shown in the following script:

**Script 32:**

```
for item in my_tuple:
    print(item)
```

**Output:**

```
James
25
Male
True
```

## § Immutability

I said earlier that tuples are immutable and cannot be modified. Let's prove it. The following script tries to update the value of the second item of the my_tuple tuple.

**Script 33:**

```
my_tuple=("James",25,"Male",True)

my_tuple[1]=30
```

In the output, you will see the following exception, which clearly says that tuple doesn't support assignment.

**Output:**

```
---------------------------------------------------------------
TypeError                          Traceback (most recent call last)
<ipython-input-75-a848a2b5dcbe> in <module>
      1my_tuple=("James",25,"Male",True)
      2
----> 3my_tuple[1]=30

TypeError: 'tuple' object does not support item assignment
```

You can try to add and remove items from a tuple, and you will see a similar exception.

### 2.2.6. Dictionaries

Dictionaries in Python store items in key-value pairs. Dictionary items are passed inside curly brackets. Each item consists of a key and a value where the key and the value are separated by a colon. Items themselves are separated via a comma.

## § Creating a Dictionary

The following script creates a dictionary country_capitals that stores country names as keys and the corresponding country capitals as values. The script then prints the country_capital dictionary along with its type.

**Script 34:**

```
country_capitals={"England":"London",
"France":"Paris",
"Japan":"Tokyo",
"China":"Beijing"}

print(country_capitals)
print(type(country_capitals))
```

**Output:**

```
{'England': 'London', 'France': 'Paris', 'Japan': 'Tokyo',
   'China': 'Beijing'}
<class 'dict'>
```

## § Accessing Dictionary Items

You can directly access a dictionary item via its index. For instance, if you execute the following script to access the first item of a dictionary, you will see an exception, as shown in the output of the script below:

**Script 35:**

```
country_capitals[0]
```

**Output:**

```
---------------------------------------------------------------
KeyError                        Traceback (most recent call last)
<ipython-input-80-0faae3a81313> in <module>
----> 1country_capitals[0]

KeyError: 0
```

A dictionary item is accessed via its key. For instance, to access the value for the item with the key *Japan*, you need to pass *Japan* as the value inside the square brackets, as shown below:

**Script 36:**

```
print(country_capitals["Japan"])
```

**Output:**

```
Tokyo
```

The items() method of a dictionary returns an iterator (collection) which can be iterated to access the keys and values of all the items in a dictionary, as shown in the following script.

**Script 37:**

```
for k,v in country_capitals.items():
    print(k+" ->"+v)
```

**Output:**

```
England ->London
France ->Paris
Japan ->Tokyo
China ->Beijing
```

To iterate through all the dictionary keys, you can use the keys() method, as shown in the following script.

**Script 38:**

```
for k in country_capitals.keys():
    print(k)
```

**Output:**

```
England
France
Japan
China
```

Similarly, to iterate through all the values in a dictionary, you can use the values() method, which returns an iterator that can be iterated using a for loop to access all the dictionary values.

**Script 39:**

```
for v in country_capitals.values():
    print(v)
```

**Output:**

```
London
Paris
Tokyo
Beijing
```

## § Adding Items to a Dictionary

To add an item to a dictionary, you have to mention a new dictionary key inside the square brackets and assign it the value you want. For instance, the following script adds a new item with the "Greece" and value "Athens" to the country_capitals dictionary.

**Script 40:**

```
country_capitals={"England":"London",
"France":"Paris",
"Japan":"Tokyo",
"China":"Beijing"}

country_capitals["Greece"]="Athens"

print(country_capitals)
```

**Output:**

```
{'England': 'London', 'France': 'Paris', 'Japan': 'Tokyo',
   'China': 'Beijing', 'Greece': 'Athens'}
```

It is important to mention that you can only have unique keys in a Python dictionary. If you add different values to the same key multiple times, the latter values will override the former values.

## § Modifying a Dictionary Item

Modifying a dictionary item is similar to adding a new item to a dictionary. Except that while modifying an item, the key for the item already exists in a dictionary. The following script modifies the value for the item with the key "Japan" in the country_capitals dictionary.

**Script 41:**

```
country_capitals={"England":"London",
"France":"Paris",
"Japan":"Tokyo",
"China":"Beijing"}

country_capitals["Japan"]="XYZ"

print(country_capitals)
```

**Output:**

```
{'England': 'London', 'France': 'Paris', 'Japan': 'XYZ',
    'China': 'Beijing'}
```

## § Deleting Dictionary Items

To delete a dictionary item, you can use the **del** keyword, followed by the dictionary name and pair of square brackets. Inside the square brackets, you need to pass the key for the item to be deleted. The following script deletes the item with the key "France" from the country_capitals dictionary.

**Script 42:**

```
country_capitals = {"England":"London",
                    "France":"Paris",
                    "Japan":"Tokyo",
                    "China":"Beijing"}

del country_capitals["France"]

print(country_capitals)
```

**Output:**

```
{'England': 'London', 'Japan': 'Tokyo', 'China': 'Beijing'}
```

Finally, you can remove all the items from a dictionary by calling the clear() function. Look at the following script for reference.

**Script 43:**

```
country_capitals={"England":"London",
"France":"Paris",
"Japan":"Tokyo",
"China":"Beijing"}

country_capitals.clear()
print(country_capitals)
```

**Output:**

```
{}
```

**Further Readings - Data Types and Variables**

To study more about Python data types and variables, see this link. (https://bit.ly/3vg9gDc)

**Hands-on Time - Exercise**

Now, it is your turn. Follow the instructions in **the exercises below** to check your understanding of the data types and variables in Python. The answers to these questions are given at the end of the book.

# Exercise 2.1

**Question 1:**

To write a multi-line string, you need to wrap a string in:

A. Double Quotes

B. Triple Quotes

C. Single Quote

D. None of the Above

**Question 2:**

The following function can be used to add an item to a tuple:

A. add()

B. insert()

C. append()

D. None of the Above

**Question 3:**

What will be the output of the following code?

```
colors ={"color1":"red",
"color2":"blue",
"color1":"green"}

print(colors["color1"])
```

A. Red

B. Blue

C. Green

D. None of the Above

## Exercise 2.2

Create a dictionary that contains days of a week(starting from Monday) as values. The keys should start from 1 with an increment of 1. Display the 3rd week of the day using its key. Use a loop to display all the key-value pairs (see the section on accessing dictionary items for reference).

# 3

# Python Operators

## 3.1. What are Python Operators?

Python operators are literal that perform different types of operations, e.g., comparing two values, assigning values to variables, adding and subtracting values, finding if an item exists in a list, etc.

Python operators can be broadly grouped into the following categories:

1. Arithmetic Operators
2. Comparison Operators
3. Assignment Operators
4. Logical Operators
5. Membership Operators
6. Identity Operators

## 3.2. Arithmetic Operators

Arithmetic operators, as the name suggests, perform arithmetic operations on the operands, for example, adding, subtracting, multiplying, and dividing numbers and variables.

Arithmetic operators in Python can be divided into 6 main categories, summarized in the following table.

| Operator Name | Operator Symbol | Functionality | Example |
|---|---|---|---|
| Addition | + | Adds the operands on either side | X= 10<br>Y = 5<br>X + Y = 15 |
| Subtraction | - | Subtracts the operands on either side | X= 10<br>Y = 5<br>X - Y = 5 |
| Multiplication | * | Multiplies the operands on either side | X= 10<br>Y = 5<br>X * Y = 50 |
| Division | / | Divides the operand on the left by the one on the right | X= 10<br>Y = 5<br>X / Y = 2 |
| Modulus | % | Divides the operand on the left by the one on the right and returns the remainder | X= 10<br>Y = 7<br>X % Y = 3 |
| Exponent | ** | Takes the exponent of the operand on the left to the power of right | X= 2<br>Y = 5<br>X % Y = 32 |

### 3.2.1. Addition Operator

The addition operator adds two or more than two operands. Here is an example:

**Script 1:**

```
X =10
Y =5

result = X + Y
print(result)
```

**Output:**

```
15
```

### 3.2.2. Subtraction Operator

The subtraction operator subtracts the operand on the right of the subtraction operator from the operand on the left side. Here is an example:

**Script 2:**

```
X =10
Y =5

result = X - Y
print(result)
```

**Output:**

```
5
```

### 3.2.3. Multiplication Operator

The multiplication operator takes the product of two or more than two operands. Here is an example:

**Script 3:**

```
X =10
Y =5

result = X * Y
print(result)
```

**Output:**

```
50
```

### 3.2.4. Division Operator

The division operator divides the operand on the left side of the division operator by the operand on the right side. Here is an example:

**Script 4:**

```
X =10
Y =5

result = X / Y
print(result)
```

**Output:**

```
2.0
```

### 3.2.5. Modulus Operator

The modulus operator divides the operand on the left side of the modulus operator by the operand on the right side and returns the remainder. Here is an example:

**Script 5:**

```
X =10
Y =7

result = X % Y
print(result)
```

**Output:**

```
3
```

### 3.2.6. Exponent Operator

The exponent operator raises the operand on the left side of the operator to the power of the operand on the right side. Here is an example:

**Script 6:**

```
X =2
Y =5

result = X ** Y
print(result)
```

**Output:**

```
32
```

## 3.3. Comparison Operators

Comparison operators compare the values contained by the operands and return a Boolean value depending upon the relationship between the operands. Comparison operators are also commonly known as *relational operators.*

The following table summarizes some of the most commonly used comparison operators in Python.

| Operator Name | Operator Symbol | Functionality | Example |
|---|---|---|---|
| Equality | == | Returns true if the values of both the operands are equal | X = 10<br>Y = 5<br>X == Y = False |
| Inequality | != | Returns true if the values of both the operands are not equal | X = 10<br>Y = 5<br>X != Y = True |

| | | | |
|---|---|---|---|
| Greater than | > | Returns true if the value of the left operand is greater than the right one | X = 10<br>Y = 5<br>X > Y =<br>True |
| Smaller than | < | Returns true if the value of the left operand is smaller than the right one | X = 10<br>Y = 5<br>X < Y =<br>False |
| Greater than or equal to | >= | Returns true if the value of the left operand is greater than or equal to the right one | X = 10<br>Y = 5<br>X >= Y =<br>True |
| Smaller than or equal to | <= | Returns true if the value of the left operand is smaller than or equal to the right one | (X = 10<br>Y = 5<br>X <= Y =<br>False |

### 3.3.1. Equality Operator

The equality operator checks for the equality between the operand on the right side and the operator on the left side and returns true if both the operands are equal. Here is an example.

**Script 7:**

```
X =2
Y =5

result = X ** Y
print(result)
```

**Output:**

```
False
```

## 3.3.2. Inequality Operator

The inequality operator checks for the inequality between the operand on the right side and the operator on the left side and returns true if both the operands are unequal. If both the operands are equal, the equality operator returns false. Here is an example.

**Script 8:**

```
X =10
Y =5
X != Y
```

**Output:**

```
True
```

## 3.3.3. Greater Than Operator

The greater than operator returns true if the operand on the left side of the greater than operator is greater than the operand on the right side. Else the operator returns false. Here is an example.

**Script 9:**

```
X =10
Y =5
X > Y
```

**Output:**

```
True
```

## 3.3.4. Smaller Than Operator

The smaller than operator returns true if the operand on the left side of the smaller than operator is smaller than the operand on the right side. Else the operator returns false. Here is an example.

**Script 10:**

```
X =10
Y =5
X < Y
```

**Output:**

```
False
```

### 3.3.5. Greater Than or Equals to Operator

The greater than or equals to operator returns true if the operand on the left side of the operator is greater or at least equals to the operand on the right side. Else the operator returns false. Look at the following example.

**Script 11:**

```
X =10
Y =5
X >= Y
```

**Output:**

```
True
```

### 3.3.6. Smaller Than or Equals to Operator

The smaller than or equals to operator returns true if the operand on the left side of the operator is smaller than or at least equals to the operand on the right side. Else the smaller than or equals to operator returns false. Look at the following example.

**Script 12:**

```
X =10
Y =5
X <= Y
```

**Output:**

```
False
```

## 3.4. Assignment Operators

Assignment operators assign values to the operand. The following table summarizes the most commonly used assignment operators in Python.

| Operator Name | Operator Symbol | Functionality | Example |
|---|---|---|---|
| Assignment | = | Used to assign the value of the right operand to the one on the left. | X = 10<br>Y = 5<br>Z = X + Y<br>assigns 15 to Z |
| Add and assign | += | Adds the operands on either side and assigns the result to the left operand | X = 10<br>Y = 5<br>X += Y<br>assigns 15 to X |
| Subtract and assign | -= | Subtracts the operands on either side and assigns the result to the left operand | X = 10<br>Y = 5<br>X -= Y<br>assigns 5 to X |
| Multiply and Assign | *= | Multiplies the operands on either side and assigns the result to the left operand | X = 10<br>Y = 5<br>X *= Y<br>assigns 50 to X |

| | | | |
|---|---|---|---|
| Divide and Assign | /= | Divides the operands on the left by the right and assigns the result to the left operand | X = 10<br>Y = 5<br>X /= Y<br>assigns 2 to X |
| Take modulus and assign | %= | Divides the operands on the left by the right and assigns the remainder to the left operand | X = 10<br>Y = 7<br>X %= Y<br>assigns 3 to X |
| Take exponent and assign | **= | Takes exponent of the operand on the left to the power of right and assign the remainder to the left operand | X = 2<br>Y = 5<br>X **= Y<br>assigns 32 to X |

## 3.4.1. Assignment

The assignment operator assigns the literal value or the value of the variable on the right side of the assignment operator to the variable on the left side of the assignment operator. Here is an example.

**Script 13:**

```
X =10
Y =5
Z = X + Y
print(Z)
```

**Output:**

```
15
```

## 3.4.2. Add and Assign

The add and assign operator adds the values of the operands on the left and right side of the operator and assigns the resultant value to the operand on the left side of the add and assign operator. Here is an example.

**Script 14:**

```
X =10
Y =5
X += Y
print(X)
```

**Output:**

```
15
```

## 3.4.3. Subtract and Assign

The subtract and assign operator is a combination of the subtraction operator and the assignment operator. The subtract and assign operator subtracts the value of the operand on the right side of the operator from the operand on the left side. The resultant value is assigned to the operand on the left side of the add and assign operator. Here is an example.

**Script 15:**

```
X =10
Y =5
X -= Y
print(X)
```

**Output:**

```
5
```

## 3.4.4. Multiply and Assign

The multiply and assign operator multiplies the values of the operands on the left and right side of the operator and assigns the resultant value to the operand on the left side of the multiply and assign operator. Here is an example.

**Script 16:**

```
X =10
Y =5
X *= Y
print(X)
```

**Output:**

```
50
```

## 3.4.5. Divide and Assign

The divide and assign operator is a combination of the division operator and the assignment operator. The divide and assign operator divides the value of the operand on the left side of the operator by the operand on the right side. The resultant value is assigned to the operand on the left side of the divide and assign operator. Here is an example.

**Script 17:**

```
X =10
Y =5
X /= Y
print(X)
```

**Output:**

```
2.0
```

## 3.4.6. Take Modulus and Assign

The take modulus and assign operator is a combination of the modulus operator and the assignment operator. The operator divides the value of the operand on the left side of the operator by the operand on the right side. The remainder value from the division is assigned to the operand on the left side of the modulus and assign operator. Here is an example.

**Script 18:**

```
X =10
Y =7
X %= Y
print(X)
```

**Output:**

```
3
```

### 3.4.7. Take Exponent and Assign

Take exponent and assign operator is a combination of exponent and assign operator where, in the first step, the operand on the left side of the exponent and assign operator is raised to the power of the operand on the right. The resultant value after taking the power is assigned to the operand on the left side of the exponent and assign operator. Look at the following example.

**Script 19:**

```
X =2
Y =5
X **= Y
print(X)
```

**Output:**

```
32
```

## 3.5. Logical Operators

Logical operators perform logical operations such as AND, OR, and NOT on the operands. The following table contains Python logical operators along with their functionalities and examples.

| Operator Name | Operator Symbol | Functionality | Example |
|---|---|---|---|
| Logical AND | and | If both the operands are true, then the condition becomes true. | X = True<br>Y = False<br>X and Y = False |
| Logical OR | or | If any of the two operands are true, then the condition becomes true. | X = True<br>Y = False<br>X or Y = True |
| Logical NOT | not | Used to reverse the logical state of its operand. | X = True<br>Y = False<br>not(X and Y) = True |

### 3.5.1. AND Operator

The AND operator performs the logical AND operation between the operands and returns true if the result of all the expressions involved in the AND operation are true. Here is an example.

**Script 20:**

```
X =True
Y =False

X and Y
```

**Output:**

```
False
```

### 3.5.2. OR Operator

The OR operator performs the logical OR operation between the operands and returns true if the result of at least one of the expressions involved in the OR operation is true. Here is an example.

**Script 21:**

```
X =True
Y =False

X or Y
```

**Output:**

```
True
```

### 3.5.3. NOT Operator

NOT operator simply reverses the output of any Boolean expression. Here is an example.

**Script 22:**

```
X =True
Y =False

not(X and Y)
```

**Output:**

```
True
```

## 3.6. Membership Operators

Membership operators check whether the value stored in the operand exists in a particular sequence or not. There are two types of membership operators in Python: 'in' and 'not in.'

The *in* operator returns true if a value is found in a particular sequence. The *not in* operator returns true in the reverse case. Take a look at the following example to see membership operators in action.

| Operator Name | Operator Symbol | Functionality | Example |
|---|---|---|---|
| in Operator | in | Returns true if an item is found inside a collection | items = [1,3,4] print( 4 in items) prints True |
| not in operator | not in | Returns true if an item is not found inside a collection | items = [1,3,4] print( 4 not in items) prints False |

### 3.6.1. The in Operator

The *in* operator returns true if an item is found inside another collection of items. Here is an example.

**Script 23:**

```
items =[1,3,4]
print(4 in items)
```

**Output:**

```
True
```

### 3.6.2. The not in Operator

The *not in* operator returns true if an item is not found inside another collection of items. Here is an example.

**Script 24:**

```
items =[1,3,4]
print(4 notin items)
```

**Output:**

```
False
```

# 3.7. Identity Operators

Identity operators are used for finding if two objects are equal by comparing memory locations.

The following table summarizes identity operators along with their descriptions and examples.

| Operator Name | Operator Symbol | Functionality | Example |
|---|---|---|---|
| is operator | is | Returns true if two objects point to same memory location | a = [“red”, “green”, “blue”]<br>b = [“red”, “green”, “blue”]<br>c = a<br>a is c<br>returns true |
| is not operator | is not | Returns true if two objects do not point to the same memory location | a = [“red”, “green”, “blue”]<br>b = [“red”, “green”, “blue”]<br>c = a<br>a is not c<br>returns false |

## 3.7.1. The Is Operator

The *is* operator returns true if two objects are equal and share the same memory locations. For instance, the following script will return TRUE since the lists a and c are equal and point to the same memory location.

**Script 25:**

```
a =["red","green","blue"]
b =["red","green","blue"]
c = a
a is c
```

**Output:**

```
True
```

## 3.7.2. The is not Operator

The *is not* operator returns true if two objects do not share the same memory locations. The two objects may have the same values, but if they do not point to the same memory location, the *is not* operator will return true.

In the following example, the *is not* operator will return FALSE since the lists a and c point to the same memory location.

**Script 26:**

```
a =["red","green","blue"]
b =["red","green","blue"]
c = a
a isnot c
```

**Output:**

```
False
```

**Further Readings - Python Operators**

To study more about Python operators, please check the official Python documentation. (https://bit.ly/3xljcx3). Get used to searching and reading this documentation. It is a great resource of knowledge.

**Hands-on Time - Exercise**

Now, it is your turn. Follow the instructions in **the exercises below** to check your understanding of the data operators in Python. The answers to these questions are given at the end of the book.

# Exercise 3.1

**Question 1:**

What will be the outcome of the following code?

```
a =["red","green","blue"]
print("red" is in a)
```

A. True

B. False

C. SyntaxError

D. red is in a

**Question 2:**

What will be the outcome of the following code?

```
X =100
Y =50

not(X is Y)
```

A. True

B. False

C. SyntaxError

D. None of the Above

**Question 3:**

Which of the following membership operators are supported by Python?

A. In

B. Out

C. Not In

D. Both A and C

# Exercise 3.2

Suppose you have the following the following three Python variables:

```
a =400
b =350
c = b
d =[100,200,300,400]
```

Perform the following tasks:

1. Show the output of a greater than b
2. Apply and operator between two logical conditions: (1) b is smaller than a, and (ii) c is b.
3. Check if b in d
4. Check if a in d
5. Check if a + b is not in d

# 4

# Decision Making and Iteration Statements in Python

This chapter covers two of the most basic programming concepts: decision-making and iteration. The decision-making and iteration are not intrinsic to Python. In every programming language, you need to make decisions based on conditions. Similarly, executing a particular piece of code multiple times with different data is also a basic programming requirement. Iteration allows you to do that.

In this chapter, you will study decision-making and iteration.

## 4.1. Conditional Statements in Python

Based on data or logic, you need to decide what piece of code to execute. This process is called decision-making in programming. Decision-making in programming is implemented via conditional statements. Conditional statements are statements that execute different pieces of code based on several conditions. There are two main types of conditional statements in Python If, else, and Elif.

### 4.1.1. If and Else Statements

The If statement is used when you want to execute a particular piece of code if a certain condition returns true. To write an If statement, you need to write the keyword *If* followed by a Boolean condition. If the Boolean condition returns true, the code that follows the If block will execute, as shown in the following example.

**Script 1:**

```
if True:
   print("The condition is true")
```

**Output:**

```
The condition is true
```

In the following example, you have two variables, x and y. The value of x is 50, and that of y is 30. The *if* condition checks if the variable x is greater than y.

**Script 2:**

```
x = 50
y = 30

if x > y:
   print("x is greater than y")
```

Since this condition in Script 2 is true, you will see the message in the output.

**Output:**

```
x is greater than y
```

Let's see another example. In the following script, we check if the value of the variable x is less than y. Since this condition returns false, the code that follows the *if* block will not execute, and you will see nothing in the output.

**Script 3:**

```
if x < y:
   print("x is less than y")
```

If you want to execute a particular piece of code, in case the *if* condition returns false, you can use the else block, as shown in the following example.

In the example below, the *if* condition checks if the value of variable x is less than y. The *if* condition will return false, and this time the code block that follows the else statement will execute.

**Script 4:**

```
if x < y:
   print("x is less than y")
else:
   print("x is greater than y")
```

**Output:**

```
x is greater than y
```

### 4.1.2. Elif Statements

If you have to check for multiple conditions in your code, you can use the elif statement in conjunction with the if and else statements. Look at the following script:

Here we have three variables x, y and z. The *if* statement checks if x is smaller than y. Next, the first *elif* statement checks if y is smaller than z. The second *elif* statement then checks if x is smaller than z. Finally, you have an *else* statement.

When the following script executes, the *if* condition is evaluated first. Since x is not smaller than y, the *if* condition will return false. Next, the first *elif* statement will execute, which also returns false since y is not smaller than z. The second *elif* statement, which evaluates if x is smaller than z, will also return false. Hence, the code block that follows the *else* statement will execute.

**Script 5:**

```
x = 50
y = 30
z = 20

if x < y:
   print("x is smaller than y")
elif y < z:
   print("y is smaller than z")
elif x < z:
   print("x is smaller than z")
else:
   print("z is the smallest integer")
```

**Output:**

```
z is the smallest integer
```

### 4.1.3. Ternary Operator

There is a shorter way of implanting conditional statements if you have only one If and Else statement. You can use the ternary operator to do so. Look at the following example. Here, the variable car contains the string, *Honda*. Next, you assign the value True to the isHonda variable if the car variable contains the string *Honda*, else the value False is assigned to the isHonda variable.

**Script 6:**

```
car = "Honda"

isHonda = True if car == "Honda" else False

print(isHonda)
```

**Output:**

```
True
```

## 4.1.4. Nesting Conditional Statements

You can write a conditional statement inside another conditional statement. Such a statement is called a nested conditional statement. Let's see an example.

In the following script, you have three variables x, y, and z. The first *if* condition checks if x is greater than y. Since this condition returns true, the code block that follows the *if* statement will execute. This code block contains nested if and else statements. The *if* statement checks if x is greater than z, which again returns true. Hence, the code block that follows the nested *if* statement executes.

**Script 7:**

```
x = 50
y = 30
z = 20

if x > y:
      print("x is greater than y")
   if x > z:
      print("x is greater than z")
   else:
      print("x is not greater than z")
```

```
elif y < z:
   print("y is smaller than z")
elif x < z:
   print("x is smaller than z")
else:
   print("z is the smallest integer")
```

Here is the output of the above script:

**Output:**

```
x is greater than y
x is greater than z
```

## 4.2. Iteration Statements in Python

In programming, oftentimes, you need to repeatedly execute a particular piece of code. Writing the same code, again and again, may render your code unmanageable. For instance, if you have to print a statement 1,000 times, you will need to write a print statement 1,000 times. Even if you copy and paste print statements, your code will grow exponentially in terms of size. This is where iteration statements come to play. With iteration statements, you can execute a code in a loop as many times as your system's memory allows you, with a few lines of code.

There are two main types of iteration statements in Python: the *for* loop and the *while* loop.

### 4.2.1. For Loop

The *for* loop is a kind of iteration *statement* that executes for a fixed number of times, which is mostly known before the *for* loop executes. Look at the following example. To start a *for* loop, you need to write the keyword *for* followed by a temporary variable that holds the current item from the collection of items on which a *for* loop iterates. For instance, in the following example, the "range(10)" function returns a collection of 10 items (0-9). In the first loop cycle, item 0 is stored in the variable i. In the second loop cycle, item 1 is stored in the variable i. Here "i" is just a variable name. You can use any other variable name as well if you want.

Since there are 10 items in the collection, the following *for* loop executes for 10 times. In each iteration, the word *hello* is printed on the console. In the output, you will see the word *hello* printed on the console.

**Script 8:**

```
for i in range(10):
    print("hello")
```

**Output:**

```
hello
hello
hello
hello
hello
hello
hello
hello
hello
hello
```

You can also confirm that the range(10) returns a collection of integers from 0 to 9 by printing the value of the "i" variable in the following script.

**Script 9:**

```
for i in range(10):
    print(i)
```

**Output:**

```
0
1
2
3
4
5
6
7
8
9
```

Let's now do something fancy. Let's try to print the table of integer 6 using a *for* loop. Here is the script which does that. Notice, here, since we do not want to start from 0, we increment i by 1 while printing the product of 6 and the value stored by the variable i.

**Script 10:**

```
for i in range(10):
    print("6 x", i+1, "= ", 6*(i+1))
```

**Output:**

```
6 x 1 =  6
6 x 2 =  12
6 x 3 =  18
6 x 4 =  24
6 x 5 =  30
6 x 6 =  36
6 x 7 =  42
6 x 8 =  48
6 x 9 =  54
6 x 10 =  60
```

If you do not want to use the item that is being iterated and you are only concerned about the number of iterations, you can skip the temporary iteration variable and replace it with an underscore. The following *for* loop executes 10 times. However, there is no temporary variable that holds the value of the item being iterated.

**Script 11:**

```
for _ in range(10):
    print("hello world")
```

**Output:**

```
hello world
hello world
hello world
hello world
hello world
hello world
hello world
hello world
hello world
hello world
```

In addition to using the range() function, which returns a collection of integers, you can also iterate over any other collection of items such as a tuple, list, or dictionary. Here is an example. Here, a *for* loop is being used to iterate through days of the week.

**Script 12:**

```
days = ["sunday", "monday", "tuesday", "wednesday",
   "thursday", "friday", "saturday"]

for d in days:
    print(d)
```

**Output:**

```
sunday
monday
tuesday
wednesday
thursday
friday
saturday
```

## 4.2.2. While Loop

The *while* loop is another type of iteration statement, which continues executing until a certain condition returns true. The syntax of a *while* loop is simple. You have to write the keyword *while* followed by a Boolean condition. For instance, in the following example, the *while* loop keeps executing until the condition j is less than 10 returns true. The condition returns true 10 times because the variable j is initialized as 0, and inside the *while* loop, it is incremented by 1 for every *while loop* iteration.

**Script 13:**

```
j = 0

while j<10:
    print("hello world")

    j = j + 1
```

**Output:**

```
hello world
hello world
hello world
hello world
hello world
```

```
hello world
hello world
hello world
hello world
hello world
```

As you did for the *for* loop, you can also use a *while* loop to print the table of an integer. Look at the following script:

**Script 14:**

```
j =0

while j<10:
print("6 x", j+1,"= ",6*(j+1))

   j = j +1
```

**Output:**

```
6 x 1 =  6
6 x 2 =  12
6 x 3 =  18
6 x 4 =  24
6 x 5 =  30
6 x 6 =  36
6 x 7 =  42
6 x 8 =  48
6 x 9 =  54
6 x 10 =  60
```

## 4.2.3. Nested Loops

Just like conditional statements, you can nest a loop inside another loop. For instance, in the following example, you have an outer *for* loop that executes 5 times. You also have an inner *for* loop that executes 5 times. Hence, the print statement will execute for a total of 5 x 5 = 25 times, as you can see from the output.

**Script 15:**

```
for i in range (5):
    for j in range (5):
        print(i ,"-",j)
```

**Output:**

```
0 - 0
0 - 1
0 - 2
0 - 3
0 - 4
1 - 0
1 - 1
1 - 2
1 - 3
1 - 4
2 - 0
2 - 1
2 - 2
2 - 3
2 - 4
3 - 0
3 - 1
3 - 2
3 - 3
3 - 4
4 - 0
4 - 1
4 - 2
4 - 3
4 - 4
```

### 4.2.4. Continue Pass and Break Statements

The continue statement is used to send the control back to the beginning of any loop. The following script prints the first 20 even integers. In the following script, you execute a loop that iterates over integers from 0 to 20. For each iteration, you check if the remainder of the integer being iterated divided by 2 is 0 or not. If the remainder is not 0, that means the integer is odd. You simply write the continue statement to return the control to the top of the loop to execute the next loop cycle. Else, the number is printed on the console.

**Script 16:**

```
for num in range(21):
    if num%2 != 0:
        continue
    else:
        print(num)
```

In the output below, you can see all even integers from 0 to 20.

**Output:**

```
0
2
4
6
8
10
12
14
16
18
20
```

The pass statement is used to simply skip the code block without doing anything. For instance, the following script prints the odd numbers between 1 and 2. The *for* loop iterates through a collection of integers from 0 to 20.

During each iteration, the number being iterated is divided by 2. If the remainder is 0, that means the number is even. The code block that follows the *if* statement is skipped using the pass statement. Else if the integer being iterated is not even, the else statement prints the integer.

**Script 17:**

```
for num in range(21):
    if num%2 == 0:
        pass
    else:
        print(num)
```

**Output:**

```
1
3
5
7
9
11
13
15
17
19
```

The break statement is used to simply break out of a loop. For instance, the *for* loop in the following script iterates through a collection of integers from 0 to 20. However, when the iterated value becomes greater than 10, the break statement stops the execution of the loop.

**Script 18:**

```
for num in range(21):

    if num%2 != 0:
        print(num)
        if num > 10:
            break
```

**Output:**

```
1
3
5
7
9
11
```

## 4.2.5. List Comprehensions in Python

Though you can iterate through a list of items using a *for* loop. There is a better way to iterate through a list using list comprehension.

Consider a scenario where you have a list of car names, and you want to filter car names with less than 5 letters in their names. You can do so using a *for* loop, as shown in the following script.

**Script 19:**

```
cars = ["Honda", "Toyota", "Ford", "BMW", "KIA", "Renault",
   "Peugeot"]

short_cars = []
for car in cars:
    if len(car) < 5:
        short_cars.append(car)

print(short_cars)
```

**Output:**

```
['Ford', 'BMW', 'KIA']
```

However, there is a smarter way to accomplish the same task as you performed in the previous script. You can use list comprehension, as shown in the following script:

### Script 20:

```
cars = ["Honda", "Toyota", "Ford", "BMW", "KIA", "Renault",
    "Peugeot"]

short_cars2 = [car for car in cars if len(car) < 5]

print(short_cars2)
```

### Output:

```
['Ford', 'BMW', 'KIA']
```

In this chapter, you studied iteration and conditional statements. In the next chapter, we will start our discussion about Functions in Python.

**Further Readings - Loops and Conditional Statements**

To study more about iteration and conditional statements in Python, please check the official Python documentation. (https://bit.ly/3enGvNW). Get used to searching and reading this documentation. It is a great resource of knowledge.

**Hands-on Time - Exercise**

Now, it is your turn. Follow the instruction in **the exercises below** to check your understanding of the iteration and conditional statements in Python. The answers to these questions are given at the end of the book.

# Exercise 4.1

**Question 1:**

You should use a *while* loop when:

A. You want to repeatedly execute a code until a certain condition returns true

B. When you know the exact number of times you want to execute a piece of code

C. To execute a code 10 times

D. None of the above

**Question 2:**

A loop defined inside another loop is called an:

A. Inner Loop

B. Nested Loop

C. Both A and B

D. None of the above

**Question 3:**

The continue statement is used in loops to:

A. Break out of the loop

B. Move to the next line of the code

C. Go back to the beginning of a loop

D. Skip two lines of code

# Exercise 4.2

Write a program that prints the prime numbers between 1 and 100.

# 5

# Functions in Python

In this chapter, you will study what Python functions are, how to define and call functions, how to pass and return values from a function, and what are some of the most common uses of functions.

## 5.1. What Are Functions?

A function is probably the most useful programming construct ever developed. A function is also commonly known as a method. In this book, you will see that both terms are used. Python development would become incredibly easier for you if you master functions.

Functions are used to encapsulate the piece of code that you have to execute multiple times, at different places in your code, with different data. For instance, if you want to implement a complex mathematical formula in your code multiple times, without functions, you will have to write the piece of code that implements the formula several times. With functions, you can write the code that implements the formula once, and whenever you need to execute that piece of code, you can call the function with a single command, and that huge piece of code will be executed.

Functions can save you not only lots of lines of code but also foster usability. A function defined in one application can be used in another application with or without modification. Finally, functions are an integral part of object-oriented programming.

## 5.2. Defining and Calling Functions

To define a function, you can use the def keyword, followed by the function name and a pair of parentheses. For instance, the following script defines a function named my_function(). The function prints a simple string on the console.

**Script 1:**

```
# defining a function named my_function
def my_function():
    print("This is my first function")
```

To execute the code inside a function, you need to call the function. To call a function, you need to specify the function name followed by the pair of parentheses. The following script calls the function my_function().

**Script 2:**

```
# calling the my_function() function
my_function()
```

When you call a function, the code inside the function definition executes. When you call the my_function() function, the print statement inside the function definition will execute, and you will see the following output:

**Output:**

```
This is my first function
```

Let's write another function that prints the table of integer 8. Look at the following script.

**Script 3:**

```
def print_eight():
    for i in range(1,11):
        print("8 x ", str(i), " = ", str(8*i))
```

Now, whenever you want to print the table of eight, instead of writing the complete logic again, you can simply call the print_eight() function, and in the output, you will see the table of the integer 8 printed on the console. Run the following script:

**Script 4:**

```
print_eight()
```

**Output:**

```
8 x  1  =  8
8 x  2  =  16
8 x  3  =  24
8 x  4  =  32
8 x  5  =  40
8 x  6  =  48
8 x  7  =  56
8 x  8  =  64
8 x  9  =  72
8 x  10  =  80
```

## 5.3. Parameterized Functions

What if you want your function to display a message of your choice instead of displaying a constant string? Or what if you want your function to print the table of the integer that you give to the function, instead of simply printing the table of integer 8, as you saw in the previous script? This is where parameterized functions come to play.

A parameterized function is a function to which you can pass data. Variables that will store the data passed to a function are called function parameters and are defined inside the parenthesis. For instance, the function in the following has one parameter, my_message. The value pass to this parameter is displayed on the console five times using a *for* loop.

**Script 5:**

```
def show_custom_message(my_message):
    for _ in range(5):
        print(my_message)
```

To call a function with parameters, in the function call, you have to pass arguments for the parameters. Arguments are values that are stored in function parameters. The following script calls the show_custom_message() function and passes a string to the my_message() parameter.

**Script 6:**

```
show_custom_message("Hello, this is a parameterized function")
```

In the output, you can see the string that you passed to the show_custom_message()five times.

**Output:**

```
Hello, this is a parameterized function
Hello, this is a parameterized function
Hello, this is a parameterized function
Hello, this is a parameterized function
Hello, this is a parameterized function
```

You can also pass multiple parameters to a function. For example, the following function accepts two parameters: my_message and count. The value passed in the my_message parameters is printed on the console for the number of times the value passed in the count parameter.

**Script 7:**

```
def show_custom_message(my_message, count):
    for _ in range(count):
        print(my_message)
```

If you run the following script, you will see a string message printed 10 times on the console. Without functions, you will have to write 10 print statements.

**Script 8:**

```
show_custom_message("Hello, this is a parameterized function",
   10)
```

**Output:**

```
Hello, this is a parameterized function
Hello, this is a parameterized function
Hello, this is a parameterized function
Hello, this is a parameterized function
Hello, this is a parameterized function
Hello, this is a parameterized function
Hello, this is a parameterized function
Hello, this is a parameterized function
Hello, this is a parameterized function
Hello, this is a parameterized function
```

Let's see another example of parameterized functions. The following script defines a function named add_numbers(), which accepts three parameter values and prints their sum on the console.

**Script 9:**

```
def add_numbers(a,b,c):
    result = a + b + c
    print(result)
```

**Script 10:**

```
add_numbers(10,12,35)
```

**Output:**

```
57
```

Finally, the following script defines the display_table() function, which prints the table of the number passed as a parameter to the display_table() function.

**Script 11:**

```
def display_table(num):
    for i in range(1,11):
        print(str(num)," x ", str(i), " = ", str(num*i))
```

Run the following script to display the table of the integer 7.

**Script 12:**

```
display_table(7)
```

**Output:**

```
7  x  1  =  7
7  x  2  =  14
7  x  3  =  21
7  x  4  =  28
7  x  5  =  35
7  x  6  =  42
7  x  7  =  49
7  x  8  =  56
7  x  9  =  63
7  x  10  =  70
```

## 5.4. Returning Values from Functions

Just like you can pass values to a function, a function can also return values.

If you do not return any value from a function, a null value is stored in the variable which stores the result of a function.

For instance, if you run the following script, the add_numbers() function will execute, and you will see the digit 57 in the output

**Script 13:**

```
def add_numbers(a,b,c):
    result = a + b + c
    print(result)

result =add_numbers(10,12,35)
```

**Output:**

```
57
```

The digit 57 is printed on the console only. It is not stored in the result variable defined outside the function. Let's print the value of the result variable to see what it contains.

**Script 14:**

```
print(result)
```

The output shows that the result contains null. This is because the add_numbers() function did not return anything.

**Output:**

```
None
```

To make a function return values, you need to use the return keyword. The values to be returned are mentioned after the return keyword. For instance, in the following script, the add_ numbers() method returns the value stored in the results variable to the function call.

**Script 15:**

```
def add_numbers(a,b,c):
    result = a + b + c
    return result # return keyword returns values

result =add_numbers(10,12,35)
```

Now, if you print the result variable, it will contain the value returned by the add_numbers() function, as shown below:

**Script 16:**

```
print(result)
```

**Output:**

```
57
```

You can also make a function return multiple values. The values are returned in the form of a tuple. The following script defines the take_cubes() method, which accepts three parameter values and returns the cube of those three values.

**Script 17:**

```
def take_cubes(a,b,c):
    a3 = a ** 3
    b3 = b ** 3
    c3 = c ** 3

    return a3, b3, c3
```

Run the following script to call the take_cubes() method with three arguments. The returned values are stored in the x, y, and z variables, which are printed on the console.

**Script 18:**

```
x, y, z =take_cubes(2,4,6)
print(x)
print(y)
print(z)
```

**Output:**

```
8
64
216
```

## 5.5. Global and Local Variables and Functions

Depending upon where they are defined, Python variables and functions can be divided into two types: Global and Local.

A variable defined outside a function or a class is called a global variable. A global variable is accessible everywhere. On the other hand, a local variable is defined inside a function. A local variable is only accessible inside a function.

The following script defines one global variable num1 and one local variable num2. The num1 variable is accessible inside the add_ten() function. Inside the function, the num1 and num2 variables are added.

**Script 19:**

```
#global variable
num1 = 10

def add_ten():
    #local variable
    num2 = 5
    result = num2 + num1

    print(result)
```

If you run the above script, you will see that no error occurs because the global variable num1 is accessible everywhere, including inside the add_ten() function.

**Script 20:**

```
add_ten()
```

**Output:**

```
15
```

In the following script, you try to access both global variable num1 and local variable num2 outside the add_ten() function.

**Script 21:**

```
#global variable
num1 = 10

def add_ten():
    #local variable
    num2 = 5
    result = num2 + num1

    print(result)

print(num1)
print(num2)
```

In the output, you will see an error that says that the num2 variable is not defined. This is because the num2 variable is a local variable inside the add_ten() function, and the Python interpreter could not find it outside the add_ten() function.

**Output:**

```
10
---------------------------------------------------------------
NameError                             Traceback (most recent call last)
<ipython-input-23-e9a560d8932e> in <module>
     10
     11 print(num1)
---> 12 print(num2)

NameError: name 'num2' is not defined
```

Similarly, a function can be local or global. A global function is not defined inside any other function, while a local function is defined inside another function. The following script defines a global function global_func() and a local function local_func(). Inside the global_func(), the local_func() is called. When you run the following script, the gloabal_func() is called first, which in return calls the local function local_func(). In the output, you will see the output of both the global_func() and local_func().

**Script 22:**

```
def global_func():
    print("This is a global function")

    def local_func():
        print("This is a local function")

#calling the local function
local_func()

#calling the global function
global_func()
```

**Output:**

```
This is a global function
This is a local function
```

Now, if you try to call the local_func() outside the global_func(), you will see an exception, as shown below:

**Script 23:**

```
#calling the local or nested function
local_func()
```

**Output:**

```
---------------------------------------------------------------
NameError                      Traceback (most recent call last)
<ipython-input-82-97bce0b6f8a0> in <module>
      1#calling the local or nested function
----> 2local_func()

NameError: name 'local_func' is not defined
```

## 5.6. Lambda Functions

A lambda function is a single-line anonymous function (a function with no name) that can accept any number of parameters and returns some value. Lambda functions are particularly useful when you want a function with a single expression.

To define a lambda function, you need to write the keyword lambda, followed by the number of parameters, a colon, and the expression. A lambda function can be stored inside a variable. To call the lambda function, you need to write the variable name followed by parenthesis. The arguments to lambda function parameters can be passed in the parenthesis.

The following script defines a lambda function with one parameter x. The function returns the square of x. The lambda function is stored in the variable square.

**Script 24:**

```
square =lambda x: x * x
```

To call the lambda function, you need to write the variable name, i.e., square, followed by the value that you want to take the square of. The following script prints the square of the integer 2.

**Script 25:**

```
print(square (2))
```

**Output:**

```
4
```

In a previous section, you saw the add_numbers() function which returns the sum of three parameter values, as shown below:

**Script 26:**

```
def add_numbers(a,b,c):
    result = a + b + c
    return result
```

The above add_numbers() function can be defined with the sum of a lambda function as follows:

**Script 27:**

```
add_numbers2 =lambda a , b, c:  a + b + c
```

**Script 28:**

```
print(add_numbers2(10,12,35))
```

**Output:**

```
57
```

You can also evaluate multiple expressions in a lambda function. The expressions have to be defined as tuple items. Each expression will return one value.

The following script defines a lambda function that takes the cube of the two parameter values.

**Script 29:**

```
cube =lambda x, y:(x **3, y**3)
print(cube(3,5))
```

**Output:**

```
(27, 125)
```

## 5.7. Recursive Functions

A recursive function is a function that calls itself. A recursive function is useful where you have to perform the same task repeatedly in a sequence. Then instead of calling a function in a loop, you can simply use recursive functions, which will keep calling themselves until a termination condition is met.

The following script creates a recursive function, which calls itself for num times, where num is a parameter passed to the function. Inside the function, you first check if the value of the num is 0. If the value is 0, the function returns. Else, the function calls itself with a value one less than num. Next, a statement is printed on the console, which tells how many times the function has been called. In the function call, a value of 7 is passed to the function. Hence, the function will call itself recursively seven times.

**Script 30:**

```
def my_func(num):
    if num == 0:
        return
    else:
    my_func(num - 1)
    print("The function is called recursively for", str(num),
    "times")

my_func(7)
```

**Output:**

```
The function is called recursively for 1 time
The function is called recursively for 2 times
The function is called recursively for 3 times
The function is called recursively for 4 times
The function is called recursively for 5 times
The function is called recursively for 6 times
The function is called recursively for 7 times
```

Recursive functions have many uses. For instance, it can be used to find a factorial of a number. A factorial of a number N is simply the product of all numbers from 1 to N.

The following script defines a function named take_fact(), which returns the factorial of the number passed to it as a parameter.

**Script 31:**

```
def take_fact(num):
    if num == 1:
        return 1
    else:
        fact = num * take_fact(num - 1)
        return fact

take_fact(8)
```

**Output:**

```
40320
```

## 5.8. Function Decorators

Function decorators are used to extend the functionality of a function without extending modifying the original function.

Before you can understand function decorators, you need to understand that a function is a variable. Just like any other variable, you can pass a function to another function as a parameter value. Also, you can define a function that returns another function.

Let's study these concepts with the help of examples.

A function can act as a variable. If you define a function and then instead of calling it, print its name, you can see the value of the function variable. The following script defines a function.

**Script 32:**

```
def my_function():
    print("This is my first function")
```

And the following script prints the function value.

**Script 33:**

```
my_function
```

**Output:**

```
<function __main__.my_function()>
```

### 5.8.1. Returning a Function

Now since you know that a function can act as a variable, a function can return a local function variable just like a normal variable.

For instance, in the following script, the outer global_func() returns the inner_func() using the return keyword.

**Script 34:**

```
def global_func():
    print("This is a global function")

    def local_func():
        print("This is a local function")

    #returning the local function
    return local_func
```

Let's call the global_func() and store the result in a variable. Run the following script.

**Script 35:**

```
my_func=global_func()
```

In the output, you will see a string on the console. This is a string printed by the print statement before the local_func() is returned inside the global_func()

**Output:**

```
This is a global function
```

If you print the my_func() variable, you will see that it contains a reference to the memory space that stores the local_func() returned by the global_func().

**Script 36:**

```
print(my_func)
```

**Output:**

```
<function global_func.<locals>.local_func at
   0x0000025310DBB670>
```

You can call a function using its variable name, just like the lambda function. For instance, to call the local_func() stored in the my_func variable, you need to add parenthesis in front of the my_func variable name. Look at the following script for reference.

**Script 37:**

```
my_func()
```

**Output:**

```
This is a local function
```

### 5.8.2. Passing a Function as a Parameter

Just as you can return a function from another function, you can also pass a function as a parameter to another function.

The following script defines two functions: function1() and function2. The function1() accepts one function as a parameter. The function1() prints a statement and then calls the function passed as a parameter to it.

**Script 38:**

```
def function1(my_func):
    print("This is from the original function")

    #calling function passed as a parameter
    my_func()
```

```
def function2():
    print("This function is passed as a parameter")
```

The following script calls the function1() and passes the function2() as a parameter to function1().

**Script 39:**

```
#passing a function as a parameter in a function call
function1(function2)
```

**Output:**

```
This is from the original function
This function is passed as a parameter
```

### 5.8.3. Creating Decorators

We are now ready to create decorators. To do so, you need to define a decorator function. The function that you want to modify is passed to this decorator function. Inside the decorator function, you define a local function called wrapper function or extended function. Once you extend the original function using a decorator function, the logic inside the wrapper or extended function will execute whenever you call the original function.

In the following script, the decorator function is named decorator_function(). The original function that will be modified is passed as a parameter original_function() to the decorator function. The wrapper or extended function that will be executed once you decorate the original_function() with the decorator_function() is defined as the extended_function().

In the following script, the extended_function() extends the functionality of the original_function() by printing a statement before and after the code logic of the original_function(). The extended_function() is called inside the decorator_function().

**Script 40:**

```
def decorator_function(orignal_function):

    def extended_function():
        print("This line executes before the original
    function")

        orignal_function()

        print("This line executes after the original
    function")

return extended_function
```

The following script defines the my_original_function() that you will modify by passing it to the decorator_function().

**Script 41:**

```
def my_original_function():
    print("This is the orignal function that is extended by
    the extended function")
```

Finally, execute the following script to call the decorator_function() and pass it the my_original_function(). The decorator function will return the extended_function(), which extends the functionality of the my_original_function()

**Script 42:**

```
extended_function=decorator_function(my_original_function)
```

You can now call the extended_function() using the extended_function().

**Script 43:**

```
extended_function()
```

**Output:**

```
This line executes before the original function
This is the original function that is extended by the extended
function
This line executes after the original function
```

Instead of passing the original function to the decorator function as a parameter, you can simply use the @ operator followed by the decorator function name before defining the original function that you want to modify, as shown in the following script.

The following script extends the my_original_function2() using the decorator_function() that you defined in a previous script.

**Script 44:**

```
@decorator_function
def my_original_function2():
    print("This function is extended using @ symbol with
   decorator")
```

**Script 45:**

```
my_original_function2()
```

Here is the output of the script above:

**Output:**

```
This line executes before the original function
This function is extended using @ symbol with decorator
This line executes after the original function
```

# 5.9. Iterators and Generators

## 5.9.1. Iterators

The iterators in Python are a collection of items that can be iterated one by one using the next(). To convert a collection into an iterator, you need to pass the collection to the iter() method. Next, you can iterate through all the items in the iterator by passing the iterator object to the next() function.

The following script creates an iterator for the colors list with four items and iterates through all four items.

**Script 46:**

```
colors =["Red","Green","Blue","Orange"]

my_iterator=iter(colors)

print(next(my_iterator))
print(next(my_iterator))
print(next(my_iterator))
print(next(my_iterator))
```

**Output:**

```
Red
Green
Blue
Orange
```

Once you iterate through all the items in an iterator and then call the next() method, you will see an error, as shown below:

**Script 47:**

```
print(next(my_iterator))
```

**Output:**

```
---------------------------------------------------------------------------
StopIteration                             Traceback (most recent call last)
      <ipython-input-112-8b90ca3bf810> in <module>
----> 1print(next(my_iterator))

StopIteration:
```

## 5.9.2. Generators

Generators are a type of iterators and return items one by one. With generators, you can create variables inside a function that always have an updated value with each function call.

A generator is defined like any other function using the def keyword. However, inside the generator, you need to use the yield keyword to specify the variable in which you want to store an updated value with each function call. The value from the yield variable can be returned by calling the __next__() function using the generator.

For instance, the following script creates a generator get_evens() which accepts one parameter. Inside the method, the value of variable x is initialized to zero. If x is less than the num parameter, the value of x is yielded and then updated.

**Script 48:**

```
def get_evens(num):

    x = 0
    while x < num:
        yield x
        x = x + 2
```

To iterate through the get_evens() generator, you need to call the generator function and then store the result in a variable.

**Script 49:**

```
nums=get_evens(11)
```

When you call the generator function for the first time using the __next__() function, x will have a value of 0, which will be returned. The value of x will be updated to 2 after the first call. The __next__() method will keep returning the next even number until the number is less than 11 (the value passed as a parameter to the get_evens() generator).

**Script 50:**

```
print(nums.__next__())
print(nums.__next__())
print(nums.__next__())
print(nums.__next__())
print(nums.__next__())
print(nums.__next__())
```

**Output:**

```
0
2
4
6
8
10
```

Once the value of the x in the get_evens() generator becomes greater than 11 and then you call the __next__() function, nothing will yield, and you will see the following error.

**Script 51:**

```
print(nums.__next__())
```

**Output:**

```
---------------------------------------------------------------------------
StopIteration                             Traceback (most recent call last)
      <ipython-input-137-6bb3b2d9d35a> in <module>
----> 1print(nums.__next__())

StopIteration:
```

You can also iterate through a generator using a *for* loop, as shown below. In this case, you don't have to call the __next__() function explicitly. Here is an example.

**Script 52:**

```
for i in get_evens(11):
    print(i)
```

**Output:**

```
0
2
4
6
8
10
```

Generators are mostly used to read large files item by item. For instance, if you have huge CSV files that won't fit into memory, you can use generators to read the file line by line, apply some process to fetched record, and then read the next line.

With this, we end our discussion on functions. In the next chapter, you will study object-oriented programming, which is one of the most fascinating programming concepts ever.

**Further Readings - Python Functions**

To study more about functions in Python, please check the official documentation. (https://bit.ly/3aDEADQ). Get used to searching and reading this documentation. It is a great resource of knowledge.

**Hands-on Time - Exercise**

Now, it is your turn. Follow the instructions in **the exercises below** to check your understanding of the Python functions. The answers to these questions are given at the end of the book.

# Exercise 5.1

**Question 1:**

A Python function can return:

A. a single value

B. multiple values

C. functions

D. all of the above

**Question 2:**

You can define multiple expressions in a lambda function using:

A. lists

B. tuples

C. dictionaries

D. None of the Above

**Question 3:**

A nested function defined inside an outer function can be:

A. accessed only inside the outer function

B. accessed anywhere in the code

C. accessed in the same class

D. all of the above

## Exercise 5.2

Write a function that calculates and prints the first N numbers of the Fibonacci series, where N is any integer.

In Fibonacci series, the next number is the sum of the previous two numbers for example:

1 = 1 = 1

2 = 1 + 0 = 1

3 = 1 + 1 = 2

4 = 2 + 1 = 3

5 = 3 + 2 = 5

6 = 5 + 3 = 8

7 = 8 + 5 = 13

8 = 13 + 8 = 21

# 6

# Object-Oriented Programming with Python

This chapter provides a brief introduction to object-oriented programming with Python. You will study what object-oriented programming is, how to create objects and classes, and how to add member methods and variables to classes. You will also see how to use classes to create custom iterators. Finally, you will study the concepts of inheritance and polymorphism in object-oriented programming.

## 6.1. What Is Object-Oriented Programming?

Object-oriented programming is a programming paradigm that models software in terms of real-world objects. The term object refers to anything that has some attributes and can perform some functions. In object-oriented programming, any independent code logic that has some attributes and can perform some functions is modeled as an object.

For instance, if you are developing a flight simulator game, you can model an airplane as an object since it has attributes like model, name, number of engines, and it also has functions such as start plane, stops the plane, moves the plane, etc. Similarly, a pilot can also be modeled as an object as he has attributes that are different from an airplane, for instance, the name, age, and gender of the pilot. Also, a pilot can have several functionalities, such as enter the plane, leave the airplane, change the seat, etc.

In the next section, you will see what objects and classes are and how they can be defined in Python.

## 6.2. Defining Classes and Creating Objects

Before you create objects, you need to create a class for that. A class can be thought of as a map or blueprint for an object. The relationship between a class and an object is similar to that of a plan and a house. By looking at the plan, you can tell how many bedrooms, dining rooms, toilets, etc., will be there in the house. Similarly, by looking at a class, you can tell the attributes and functionalities of an object. You can create multiple objects using a single class.

To create a class, you have to use the keyword *class* followed by the class name and a semicolon. The following script creates a class named NewClass with one function named class_method().

**Script 1:**

```
## defining a class
class NewClass:


    def class_method(self):

        print("Hello this is a method inside a class")
```

To create an object of a class, you need to write the class name followed by a pair of parentheses. The following script creates an object named nc for the class NewClass. Using the nc object, you can call the functions (methods) of the new class. To do so, you need to append a dot operator followed by the name, as shown below:

**Script 2:**

```
#creating a class object
nc=NewClass()

#calling a method using class object
nc.class_method()
```

## 6.3. Declaring Methods and Variables in a Class

As I said earlier, an object can have attributes and methods. To create an object with attributes and functions, you need to add those attributes and methods to the corresponding class. Attributes and methods defined inside a class are called member attributes and member methods. Remember, a method is another name used for functions.

The following script creates a class with one member method class_method() and two member attributes color and id. In Python, you need to pass self as the first attribute for instance methods. An instance method is a method that can be accessed using a class object. Similarly, to create instance variables, you need to define those variables inside an instance method, and you have to prefix the keyword *self* before the attribute names.

### Script 3:

```
## defining a class
class NewClass:

    def class_method(self):

        #class member variables
        self.color = "red"
        self.id = 24

        print("Hello this is a method inside a class")
```

The following script creates an object of the NewClass class and calls the member method class_method().

Note: An object is also called an instance.

### Script 4:

```
#creating a class object
nc1 =NewClass()

#calling a method using class object
nc1.class_method()
```

### Output:

```
Hello this is a method inside a class
```

Similarly, in the following script, the member attributes of the NewClass class are accessed and printed via the nc1 object.

### Script 5:

```
#accessing class members
print(nc1.color)
print(nc1.id)
```

### Output:

```
red
24
```

As I said earlier, you can create multiple objects from a single class. In the following script, you define another object nc2 using the same NewClass class and access the member method and member attributes of the class.

**Script 6:**

```
#creating a class object
nc2 =NewClass()

#calling a method using class object
nc2.class_method()

#accessing class members
print(nc2.color)
print(nc2.id)
```

**Output:**

```
Hello this is a method inside a class
red
24
```

In the previous sections, you created two objects: nc1 and nc2 using the class NewClass. The values for color and id attributes for both objects were the same. In real-life scenarios, most of the time, the values for instance members of different objects of the same class will be different.

Let's create a class where the member method class_method() accepts two parameter values that are used to assign values to the color and id attributes. Look at the following script.

**Script 7:**

```
## defining a class
class NewClass:

    #declaring a function with parameters
    def class_method(self, my_color, my_id):
```

```
        #class member variables
        self.color = my_color
        self.id = my_id

        print("Hello this is a method inside a class")
```

Let's create an object of the NewClass class. While calling the class_method() method of the class, you can pass values for the color and id attributes, as shown below:

**Script 8:**

```
#creating a class object
nc1 =NewClass()

#calling a method using class object
nc1.class_method("Yellow",25)

#accessing class members
print(nc1.color)
print(nc1.id)
```

**Output:**

```
Hello this is a method inside a class
Yellow
25
```

Next, you can create another object of the NewClass class and assign different values to the color and id attributes by passing the values to the class_method().

**Script 9:**

```
#creating a class object
nc2 =NewClass()

#calling a method using class object
nc2.class_method("Green",30)
```

```
#accessing class members
print(nc2.color)
print(nc2.id)
```

**Output:**

```
Hello this is a method inside a class
Green
30
```

You can now see that the nc1 and nc2 objects have different values for color and id attributes.

## 6.4. Class Constructors

A constructor is a function that is automatically called when you create an object of a class. The name of the constructor function will always be __init__().

**Note:** Creating an object of a class is also known as initializing a class.

The following script creates a class with a constructor method that accepts two parameter values, which are used to initialize the color and id attributes. The class also contains a method display_vars(), which displays values of the color and id attributes.

**Script 10:**

```
class NewClass:

    def __init__(self, my_color, my_id):

        #class member variables
        self.color = my_color
        self.id = my_id

```

```
    def display_vars(self):
        print(self.color)
        print(self.id)
```

When you create an object of a class having a custom constructor, you need to pass the values for the constructor parameter using the parenthesis that follows the class name. The following script creates an object nc1 for the NewClass class. The values passed to the constructor are *Purple* and 50. These values will be respectively assigned to the color and id attributes of the nc1 object. You can see that using a constructor, you can initialize member attributes without defining any extra method.

**Script 11:**

```
#creating a class object
#passing values to class constructor
nc1 =NewClass("Purple",50)

#calling a method using class object
nc1.display_vars()
```

**Output:**

```
Purple
50
```

The following script creates another object for the NewClass class and initializes the member attributes via a constructor.

**Script 12:**

```
#creating a class object
#passing values to class constructor
nc1 =NewClass("Pink",100)

#calling a method using class object
nc1.display_vars()
```

**Output:**

```
Pink
100
```

You can see that constructor makes your life much easier, especially when you want to initialize some member attributes at the time of object initialization.

## 6.5. Class Members vs. Instance Members

It is extremely important to understand the difference between class members attributes and methods and instance members attributes and methods in object-oriented programming in Python.

A class attribute is an attribute that can be accessed via the class name, and its value is shared among different objects. A class attribute is declared outside of the constructor.

An instance attribute, on the other hand, is an attribute that is intrinsic to an instance (object) and is not shared among different objects of a class. Each object of a class has its copy of an instance variable. Instance attributes can only be accessed via instance names. Instance attributes are declared inside an instance method.

Similarly, a class method is a method that can be accessed via a class name. A class method doesn't contain any parameter value.

On the other hand, an instance method is called using the instance name. The first parameter of the instance object will always be the keyword self, which refers to the object from which the method is being called.

The following script creates a new class named NewClass with one class attribute num_objects and two instance attributes color and id. The class also contains a constructor, a class method show_object_counts(), and an instance method display_vars().

Whenever an object of the NewClass class is created, the constructor initializes the values of the instance attributes: color and id. The constructor also increments the value of the class attributes num_objects by 1. The instance method display_vars() displays the values of the instance attributes color and id. The class method show_object_counts() displays the value of the object counts variable.

**Script 13:**

```
class NewClass:

    ## class variable
    num_objects = 0

    ## constructor
    def __init__(self, my_color, my_id):

        #class member variables
        self.color = my_color
        self.id = my_id
        NewClass.num_objects +=1

    ## instance method
    def display_vars(self):
        print(self.color)
        print(self.id)

    ## class method
    def show_object_counts():
        print("Number of objects:", str(NewClass.num_objects))
```

When you create the first object of the NewClass class, the value of the num_objects will be incremented to 1, as shown in the following script.

**Script 14:**

```
#creating a class object
nc1 =NewClass("Purple",50)

#calling instance method
nc1.display_vars()

#calling class method
NewClass.show_object_counts()
```

**Output:**

```
Purple
50
Number of objects: 1
```

Now, when you create another object of the NewClass class, the value of class variable num_objects will be incremented to 2 since it is shared between all the objects, and previously it had a value of 1. Execute the following script to see this for yourself.

**Script 15:**

```
#creating a class object
nc2 =NewClass("Pink",100)

#calling instance method
nc2.display_vars()

#calling class method
NewClass.show_object_counts()
```

**Output:**

```
Pink
100
Number of objects: 2
```

## 6.6. Create Iterators Using Classes

In the previous chapter, you saw how iterators can be used to iterate over a collection one by one using the next() method. Using classes, you can create your custom iterator, as well. You need to define two methods inside a class to create an iterator: __iter__() and __next__(). The initial value of the iterator is assigned inside the __iter__() method. The value is incremented or updated inside the __next__() method. The following script creates an iterator Get_Evens, which starts from 2 and returns the next even number whenever the next() method is called on it.

**Script 16:**

```
class Get_Evens:

    def __iter__(self):

        #initiliaze an iterator value
        self.id = 2

        #return iterator class object
        return self

    def __next__(self):

        #save the previous iterator value
        new_id = self.id
```

```
        #assign next value
        self.id +=2

        #return the previous iterator value
        return new_id
```

The following script creates an object of the Get_Evens class, converts it into an iterator by calling the iter() method, and prints the first iterator value via the next() method.

**Script 17:**

```
get_evens=Get_Evens()

get_evens_iter=iter(get_evens)
print(next(get_evens_iter))
```

**Output:**

```
2
```

You can keep calling the next() method to get the next iterator value, as shown in the following script:

**Script 18:**

```
print(next(get_evens_iter))
print(next(get_evens_iter))
print(next(get_evens_iter))
print(next(get_evens_iter))
print(next(get_evens_iter))
```

**Output:**

```
4
6
8
10
12
```

You can also use a *for* loop to iterate through your custom iterator. You just have to call the next() method on the iterator inside the *for* loop. Look at the following script for reference.

**Script 19:**

```
get_evens = Get_Evens()

get_evens_iter = iter(get_evens)
for _ in range(10):
    print(next(get_evens_iter))
```

**Output:**

```
2
4
6
8
10
12
14
16
18
20
```

# 6.7. Inheritance in Python

Inheritance allows a class to inherit the characteristics, e.g., member methods and attributes of another class. A class that inherits another class is called a child class. On the other hand, a class inherited by another class is called a parent class. A child can inherit from multiple parent classes, while a parent class can be inherited from multiple child classes.

## 6.7.1. A Simple Example of Inheritance

Let's see a simple example of inheritance in Python. In the following script, you define a Parent class with one method display_text(). You also declare a child class named Child that inherits the Parent class. You can see that to inherit from a class, you simply have to pass the parent class name inside the parenthesis that follows the child class name.

**Script 20:**

```
class Parent:

    def display_text(self):
        self.id = 10
        print("A function inside the parent class")

class Child(Parent):
    pass
```

Let's create an object of the Child class and call the display_text() method.

**Script 21:**

```
child = Child()
child.display_text()
print(child.id)
```

**Output:**

```
A function inside the parent class
10
```

The output shows that you were able to successfully call the display_text() method from the Child class object, although the display_text() method is not defined inside the Child class. However, since the Child class inherits the Parent class, which contains the display_text() method, you can call the method using the Child class object.

### 6.7.2. An Advanced Example of Inheritance

The child and parent classes have an *is-a* relationship between them. The basic idea behind inheritance is that the member attributes and methods common between various classes can be grouped inside the parent class, and the members and attributes intrinsic to child classes can be implemented inside child classes.

Let's see an advanced example of inheritance. The following script creates a class named Shape with two attributes, name and area, and one method display_shape_attr().

**Script 22:**

```
class Shape:

    def set_shape_attr(self, name, area):
        self.shape_name = name
        self.area = area

    def display_shape_attr(self):
        print("The shape name is ", self.shape_name)
        print("The shape area is ", self.area)
```

Let's create two child classes from the Shape class. The first class that we are going to create is a Circle class that has its attribute radius and a method that displays the value of the radius attribute. Notice the relationship between the Circle and Shape class is *is-a*, as a Circle is-a Shape.

**Script 23:**

```
class Circle(Shape):

    def set_circle_attr(self, radius):
        self.radius = radius

    def display_circle_attr(self):
        print("The radius of the circle is ", self.radius)
```

Let's create another class named Square, which inherits the Shape class. The Square class has one attribute vertices and a method, which displays the value of the vertices attribute.

**Script 24:**

```
class Square(Shape):

    def set_square_attr(self, vertices):
        self.vertices = vertices

    def display_square_attr(self):
        print("Total number of vertices in a square ", self.
    vertices)
```

You can see that both Circle and Square classes have two common attributes name and area. The common attributes are implemented in the parent Shape class. The specific attributes, i.e., radius and vertices, are implemented in Circle and Square classes, respectively.

The following script creates objects of the Circle class and displays the value of the name, area, and radius attributes.

**Script 25:**

```
#creating a child class object
circle = Circle()
```

```
#calling parent class methods
circle.set_shape_attr("Circle",200)
circle.display_shape_attr()

#calling child class methods
circle.set_circle_attr(500)
circle.display_circle_attr()
```

**Output:**

```
The shape name is  Circle
The shape area is  200
The radius of the circle is  500
```

Similarly, the following script creates an object of the Square class and displays the value of name, area, and vertices attributes.

**Script 26:**

```
#creating a child class object
square = Square()

#calling parent class methods
square.set_shape_attr("Sqauare",300)
square.display_shape_attr()

#calling child class methods
square.set_square_attr(4)
square.display_square_attr()
```

**Output:**

```
The shape name is  Square
The shape area is  300
Total number of vertices in a square  4
```

### 6.7.3. Calling Parent Class Constructor via a Child Class

You can define constructors in both parent and child classes. You can then initialize the parent class constructor using the child class constructor. Let's see an example.

The following script defines a parent class named Shape.

**Script 27:**

```
class Shape:

    def __init__(self, name, area):
        self.shape_name = name
        self.area = area

    def display_shape_attr(self):
        print("The shape name is ", self.shape_name)
        print("The shape area is ", self.area)
```

The following script defines a child class Circle that inherits the parent class Shape. Look at the constructor of the Circle class. It accepts three parameters name, area, and radius. Inside the constructor, the super() keyword is used to refer to the parent class. The parent class constructor is called using super().__init__() method and the values for the name and area parameters are passed to the parent class constructor. The third parameter initializes the child class attribute, i.e., radius.

**Script 28:**

```
class Circle(Shape):

    def __init__(self, name, area, radius):
        #calling parent class constructor
```

```
        super().__init__(name, area)
        self.radius = radius

    def display_circle_attr(self):
        print("The radius of the circle is ", self.radius)
```

Now, when you create an object of the Circle class, you pass three parameter values. The first two parameter values will initialize the parent class attributes: name and area, while the third parameter will initialize the child class attribute, radius.

**Script 29:**

```
#creating a child class object
circle = Circle("Circle",700,400)

#calling parent class methods
circle.display_shape_attr()

#calling child class methods
circle.display_circle_attr()
```

**Output:**

```
The shape name is  Circle
The shape area is  700
The radius of the circle is  400
```

### 6.7.4. Polymorphism

Polymorphism is one of the most exciting concepts of inheritance. With polymorphism, you can make the same function act differently.

For instance, consider the example of the method in the following script. The method accepts two mandatory parameter values, a and b, and one optional parameter c, whose default value is 0.

When you pass the value for the three parameters, the sum of three parameter values will be returned. If you pass two values, c will be assigned the value of c. If the value of the parameter c is zero, you subtract b from a and return the value.

**Script 30:**

```
def my_func(a,b,c = 0):
    if c == 0:
        return a - b
    else:
        return a + b + c
```

Let's call the my_func() method with two and three parameters.

**Script 31:**

```
print(my_func(10,22,20))
print(my_func(15,10))
```

The output shows that when you pass three parameters to the my_func() function, the sum of three parameters is returned. Else if you pass two parameters, the second parameter value is subtracted from the first, and the result is returned.

**Output:**

```
52
5
```

You can also implement polymorphism via inheritance. To do so, you need to override the methods implemented in the parent class. Overriding a method means having a method with the same name in parent and child classes. In that case, a child class overrides a parent class method. When you call that method using a child class object, the child class implementation of the method will be executed.

Here is an example. The following script defines a class named Shape with a method display_shape_attr().

**Script 32:**

```
class Shape:

    def __init__(self, name, area):
        self.shape_name = name
        self.area = area

    def display_shape_attr(self):
        print("The shape name is ", self.shape_name)
        print("The shape area is ", self.area)
```

The child class Circle inherits the parent Shape class. However, the child class overrides the display_shape_attr() method and provides its own implementation.

**Script 33:**

```
class Circle(Shape):

    def __init__(self, name, area, radius):
        super().__init__(name, area)
        self.radius = radius

#overriding display_shape_attr() method of the parent class
    def display_shape_attr(self):
        print("The shape name is ", self.shape_name)
        print("The shape area is ", self.area)
        print("The radius of the circle is ", self.radius)
```

Similarly, the Square class in the following script inherits the Shape class but provides its implementation for the display_shape_attr() method.

**Script 34:**

```
class Square(Shape):

    def __init__(self, name, area, vertices):
        super().__init__(name, area)
        self.vertices = vertices

#overriding display_shape_attr() method of the parent class
    def display_shape_attr(self):
        print("The shape name is ", self.shape_name)
        print("The shape area is ", self.area)
        print("Total number of vertices in a square ", self.
   vertices)
```

Now, if you create objects of Shape, Circle, and Square classes and call the display_shape_attr() method, you will see that the corresponding objects execute their implementation of the display_shape_attr(). In other words, depending upon the Class, a method with the same name is used to implement different logics, which is polymorphism.

**Script 35:**

```
shape= Shape("Shape",500)
circle= Circle("Circle",700,400)
square = Square("Square",500,4)



shape.display_shape_attr()
print("===================================")
circle.display_shape_attr()
print("===================================")
square.display_shape_attr()
```

**Output:**

```
The shape name is  Shape
The shape area is  500
===================================
The shape name is  Circle
The shape area is  700
The radius of the circle is  400
===================================
The shape name is  Square
The shape area is  500
Total number of vertices in a square  4
```

**Further Readings - Object-Oriented Programming**

To study more about object-oriented programming in Python, please check the official documentation (https://bit.ly/2S3vHgH). Get used to searching and reading this documentation. It is a great resource of knowledge.

**Hands-on Time - Exercise**

Now, it is your turn. Follow the instructions in **the exercises below** to check your understanding of object-oriented programming in Python. The answers to these questions are given at the end of the book.

# Exercise 6.1

**Question 1:**

What is true for Python:

A. A child can inherit from only one parent class

B. A parent class can only have one child class

C. A child class can inherit from multiple parent classes

D. None of the Above

**Question 2:**

An instance method can be accessed via:

A. class name

B. class and object names

C. object name

D. All of the above

**Question 3:**

Which of the following method is used to call the parent class constructor in Python?

A. parent()

B. base()

C. super()

D. object()

## Exercise 6.2

Perform the following tasks:

1. Create a Parent class Vehicle with two instance attributes: name and price, and one instance method show_vehicle(). The show_vehicle() method displays the name and price attributes.
2. Initialize the Vehicle class attributes using a constructor.
3. Create a class Car that inherits the Parent Vehicle class. Add an attribute named tires to the Car class. Override the show_vehicle() method of the parent Vehicle class and display name, price, and tire attributes.
4. Inside the Car class constructor, call the Vehicle class constructor and pass the name and price to the parent Vehicle class constructor.
5. Create objects of Car and Vehicle classes, and call show_vehicle() method using both objects.

# 7

# Exception Handling with Python

Your python code, like any other programming language, is likely to come across different types of errors and exceptions. Broadly, the errors in a Python application will be divided into two types: compile-time errors and runtime errors. Compile-time errors occur before an application is executed, while runtime errors occur during application execution. Runtime errors are also called exceptions and are likely to crash the application. Since Python is a loosely-typed language where data type is evaluated at runtime, it is much more likely to throw exceptions than strongly typed languages such as Java and C#.

In this chapter, you will see how to handle exceptions in Python. Exceptions handling can be defined as the process of managing exceptions without letting the application crash at runtime. The exception handling further allows you to display more readable messages to users regarding what caused your application to behave abnormally and what can be done to perform the task that a user wants to perform using the application. So let's begin without further ado.

## 7.1. What Are Exceptions?

Before you see an example of an exception or a runtime error, let's first see how a compile-time error looks. Execute the following script:

**Script 1:**

```
# a function which divides two numbers
def divide_numbers[a, b]:
    result = a / b
    print(result)
```

The above script will not be executed because it cannot be interpreted by the Python interpreter. The output shows that the code has syntax errors since function parameters are specified in square brackets in the above script. You need to specify function parameters in round brackets. You can see that a compile-time error is caught at runtime.

**Output:**

```
File "<ipython-input-3-cb29fff5ffe2>", line 2
   def divide_numbers[a, b]:
                     ^

SyntaxError: invalid syntax
```

Let's now see an example of a runtime error or an exception. The following script defines a function that accepts two parameters, a and b, and returns the result when variable a is divided by variable b. If you execute the following script, you will see no error.

**Script 2:**

```
# a function which divides two numbers
def divide_numbers(a, b):
    result = a / b
    print(result)
```

Let's now call the above function with parameter values 20 and 0. Run the following script.

**Script 3:**

```
divide_numbers(20,0)
```

When you run the above script, an error will occur, which says that you cannot divide a number by zero. You can see that the error only occurs when you pass 0 as the value for the parameter b. Otherwise, this error will never occur. This is an example of an exception.

**Output:**

```
---------------------------------------------------------------
ZeroDivisionError              Traceback (most recent call last)
      <ipython-input-5-888fe953dc7d> in <module>
----> 1divide_numbers(20,0)

      <ipython-input-4-e4f20ab09acc> in divide_numbers(a, b)
      1# a function which divides two numbers
      2def divide_numbers(a, b):
----> 3result = a / b
      4 print(result)

ZeroDivisionError: division by zero
```

In the next section, you will see how to handle such exceptions.

## 7.2. Handling Multiple Exceptions

A Python script can pass through different types of exceptions. For instance, the following script can through two exceptions. It will pass through a division by zero exception if you pass 0 as the value for the parameter b. If you pass a non-zero value for b, the following script will still through an exception in the following script you are printing value for the variable "result_new," which is not initialized.

**Script 4:**

```
def divide_numbers(a, b):
    result = a / b
    print(result_new)
```

Run the following script to see the zero division exception.

**Script 5:**

```
divide_numbers(20,0)
```

**Output:**

```
---------------------------------------------------------------
ZeroDivisionError                Traceback (most recent call last)
<ipython-input-7-888fe953dc7d> in <module>
----> 1divide_numbers(20,0)

<ipython-input-6-25da363128b6> in divide_numbers(a, b)
      1defdivide_numbers(a, b):
----> 2result = a / b
      3     print(result_new)
      4

ZeroDivisionError: division by zero
```

Let's now pass a non-zero value for the variable b, i.e., 10, as shown in the following script.

**Script 6:**

```
divide_numbers(20,10)
```

When you run the above script, you will see a NameError exception since the variable "result_new" is not defined before it is used.

**Output:**

```
---------------------------------------------------------------------
NameError                          Traceback (most recent call last)
<ipython-input-8-9a888e62bc4b> in <module>
----> 1divide_numbers(20,10)

<ipython-input-6-25da363128b6> in divide_numbers(a, b)
      1defdivide_numbers(a, b):
      2     result = a / b
----> 3print(result_new)
      4

NameError: name 'result_new' is not defined
```

So, you can see that one python script can generate multiple exceptions.

To handle exceptions in Python, you need to wrap the code, which is most likely to through an exception, inside a try block. A try block must follow by an except block. The except block contains the code which you want to execute in case an exception occurs. Look at the following script.

Here inside the divide_numbers() method, the code where a is divided by b and where the result_new variable is printed is wrapped inside the try block. In case an exception occurs, a message is displayed to the user that "an exception occurred."

**Script 7:**

```
def divide_numbers(a, b):
    try:
        result = a / b
        print(result_new)
    except:
        print("an exception occurred")
```

Now, if you execute the following script, a division by zero exception will occur.

**Script 8:**

```
divide_numbers(20,0)
```

However, since you have no handled the exception, you will see the following message from the except block.

**Output:**

```
an exception occurred
```

Similarly, if you pass a non-zero value for the parameter b, the NameError exception will occur. However, as you have also handled that exception, you will see the message that "an exception occurred."

**Script 9:**

```
divide_numbers(20,10)
```

**Output:**

```
an exception occurred
```

In the previous script, you received the same message for both the exception. You can print different messages for different exceptions as well. When an exception is thrown, an object of the Exception class is created. In the except block, you can use that object to print the exception message, as shown in the following script.

**Script 10:**

```
def divide_numbers(a, b):
    try:
        result = a / b
        print(result_new)
    except Exception as e:
        print(e)
```

Again execute the following script. You will that "division by zero" will be printed on the console.

**Script 11:**

```
divide_numbers(20,0)
```

**Output:**

```
division by zero
```

And if you execute the following script, the name error exception will occur, and you will see the corresponding error message in the output.

**Script 12:**

```
divide_numbers(20,10)
```

**Output:**

```
name 'result_new' is not defined
```

## 7.3. Individually Handling Different Exceptions

In the previous section, you saw how to handle all the exceptions using a single try and except block. You can individually handle different exceptions and execute different codes in the except block based on the exception type. In the following script, you have two except blocks to catch NameError exception and ZeroDivisionError exception.

**Script 13:**

```
def divide_numbers(a, b):
    try:
        result = a / b
        print(result_new)
#catching name error exception
    except NameError:
        print("One of your variables is not initialized before
    usage")
#catching divide by zero exception
    except ZeroDivisionError:
        print("Division of a number by zero is not possible")
```

Now, when the ZeroDivsisionError occurs, you will see the corresponding except block execute. Run the following script to see this effect.

**Script 14:**

```
divide_numbers(20,0)
```

You can see from the output below that the except block for the ZeroDivisionError is executed, and the corresponding statement is printed.

**Output:**

```
Division of a number by zero is not possible
```

Similarly, if you execute the following script, you will see that the NameError exception will occur, and the except block that handles the NameError exception will execute.

**Script 15:**

```
divide_numbers(20,10)
```

**Output:**

```
One of your variables is not initialized before usage
```

## 7.4. The Finally and Else Block

The finally block is always executed whether or not an exception occurs. The finally block is normally used to clear up any memory spaces. In the following script, you added a finally block at the end of the divide_numbers() method.

**Script 16:**

```
def divide_numbers(a, b):
    try:
        result = a / b
        print(result)

#catching name error exception
    except NameError:
        print("One of your variable is not initialized before
    usage")

#catching divide by zero exception
    except ZeroDivisionError:
        print("Division of a number by zero is not possible")
    finally:
        print("this will be called in any case")
```

Execute the following script.

**Script 17:**

```
divide_numbers(20,0)
```

In the output, you will see the output from the except block that catches the ZeroDivisionError exception. The output also shows that the print statement inside the finally block is also executed.

**Output:**

```
Division of a number by zero is not possible
this will be called in any case
```

Let's see another example of how the finally block works. If you run the following script, no exception will occur. However, the finally block will still execute, and you will see the output from the print statement inside the finally block in the console output.

**Script 18:**

```
divide_numbers(20,10)
```

**Output:**

```
2.0
this will be called in any case
```

The else block can be used when you want to execute an alternate piece of script in case if exception does not occur.

**Script 19:**

```
def divide_numbers(a, b):
    try:
        result = a / b
        print(result)
    except NameError:
        print("One of your variable is not initialized before
  usage")
    else:
        print("The exception did not occur")
    finally:
        print("this will be called in any case")
```

For instance, if you run the following script, no exception will occur, and therefore, the code block that follows the else statement will execute, along with the finally block.

**Script 20:**

```
divide_numbers(20,10)
```

**Output:**

```
2.0
The exception did not occur
this will be called in any case
```

## 7.5. User-Defined Exceptions

In addition to default Python exceptions, you can define your custom exceptions. The simplest way to raise a custom exception is by using the "raise Exception" keywords. The message for an exception is passed to the constructor of the Exception class.

The following script throws an exception if you try to insert more than 3 items in the list variable my_list. Since the following script adds 4 items to the my_list, you will see an exception as shown in the output of the following script.

**Script 21:**

```
my_list = []

for _ inrange (4):

    my_list.append("Hello world")
    print(my_list)
    if len(my_list) > 3:
        raiseException("This list cannot contain more than 3 
items")
```

**Output:**

```
['Hello world']
['Hello world', 'Hello world']
['Hello world', 'Hello world', 'Hello world']
['Hello world', 'Hello world', 'Hello world', 'Hello world']
--------------------------------------------------------------
Exception                            Traceback (most recent call last)
<ipython-input-23-abf5e138e53f> in <module>
      6     print(my_list)
      7iflen(my_list)>3:
----> 8raise Exception("This list cannot contain more than 3
    items")
      9

Exception: This list cannot contain more than 3 items
```

The exception defined in the previous script was named Exception. You can define your custom-named exception by creating a class that inherits from the Exception class.

In the following script, you define a class for a custom exception named ListItemOverFlow, which inherits from the Exception class. In your custom class constructor, you pass your custom error message to the superclass constructor.

**Script 22:**

```
class ListItemOverFlow(Exception):
    """Exception raised when more than 3 items are added in a
    list

    Attributes:
        new_list -- the list itself
        error_message -- the detail of the exception
    """
```

```
# the constructor of the child ListItemOverFlow class
    def __init__(self, new_list, error_message="Exception:
    This list cannot contain more than 3 items"):
        self.new_list = new_list
        self.error_message = error_message
        super().__init__(self.error_message)
```

Now when you throw the ListItemOverFlow exception, you will see your named exception in the output along with the custom message that you defined inside the ListItemOverFlow class constructor. Look at the following script for reference.

**Script 23:**

```
my_list = []

for _ inrange (4):

    my_list.append("Hello world")
    print(my_list)
    if len(my_list) > 3:
        raise ListItemOverFlow(my_list)
```

**Output:**

```
['Hello world']
['Hello world', 'Hello world']
['Hello world', 'Hello world', 'Hello world']
['Hello world', 'Hello world', 'Hello world', 'Hello world']
---------------------------------------------------------------
ListItemOverFlow              Traceback (most recent call last)
<ipython-input-25-0c8b4be4df9c> in <module>
      6     print(my_list)
      7iflen(my_list)>3:
----> 8raiseListItemOverFlow(my_list)

ListItemOverFlow: Exception: This list cannot contain more
   than 3 items
```

The error message that you pass to the super class constructor is printed by the str() method of the super class. You can modify the error message further by overriding the str() method of the super class. For instance, in the following script, the number of items in the list and the error message are displayed via the str() method.

**Script 24:**

```
class ListItemOverFlow(Exception):
    """Exception raised when more than 3 items are added in a
   list

   Attributes:
       new_list -- the list itself
       error_message -- the detail of the exception
   """

    def __init__(self, new_list, error_message="Exception:
   This list cannot contain more than 3 items"):
        self.new_list = new_list
        self.error_message = error_message
        super().__init__(self.error_message)

#this method will be called when the ListItemOverFlow
exception occurs
    def __str__(self):
    return f'{len(self.new_list)} -> {self.error_message}'
```

Now, if you write the following script and throw the ListItemOverFlow exception, you will see the number of items, i.e., 4, and the error message in the exception, as shown in the output of the following script.

**Script 25:**

```
my_list = []

for _ inrange (4):

    my_list.append("Hello world")
    print(my_list)
    if len(my_list) > 3:
        raise ListItemOverFlow(my_list)
```

**Output:**

```
['Hello world']
['Hello world', 'Hello world']
['Hello world', 'Hello world', 'Hello world']
['Hello world', 'Hello world', 'Hello world', 'Hello world']
---------------------------------------------------------------------------
ListItemOverFlow                          Traceback (most recent call last)
<ipython-input-27-0c8b4be4df9c> in <module>
      6     print(my_list)
      7iflen(my_list)>3:
----> 8raiseListItemOverFlow(my_list)

ListItemOverFlow: 4 -> Exception: This list cannot contain
   more than 3 items
```

The user-defined or the custom exceptions are handled in the same way as you handle default Python exceptions. In the next chapter, you will see how to do input and output tasks in Python.

**Further Readings - Exception Handling in Python**

To study more about exception handling in Python, please check the official documentation. (https://bit.ly/2QRHm1s). Get used to searching and reading this documentation. It is a great resource of knowledge.

**Hands-on Time - Exercise**

Now, it is your turn. Follow the instruction in **the exercises below** to check your understanding of exception handling in Python. The answers to these questions are given at the end of the book.

# Exercise 7.1

**Question 1:**

What is the minimum number of try and except blocks required to catch all the exceptions in Python?

A. 1

B. Equal to the number of all exceptions in Python

C. 2

D. None of the Above

**Question 2:**

To create a user-defined exception, you have to create a class that inherits from the following class:

A. Error

B. Exception

C. Try

D. Catch

**Question 3:**

Exception handling is important because it:

A. Saves your program from crashing at runtime

B. Helps display custom messages to the user in case of an error

C. Speeds up program execution

D. Both A and B

## Exercise 7.2

Create a custom exception named EvenNumberInsertionException, which tells users that they cannot add an even number in a list of integers. Create a list and add some odd and even numbers to it. Raise the EvenNumberInsertionException and tell the user the even number added along with the error message.

# 8

# Reading and Writing Data from Files and Sockets

You will often need to import data from different types of files into your Python application. For instance, if you are developing a natural language processing application that classifies spam emails, you might need to train your classifier model using text files that contain spam emails. Furthermore, you might need to read data from CSV files and write data to CSV files. Finally, in addition to reading and writing data to flat files, you might also need to send and receive data over the network using sockets.

In this chapter, you will see how to read and write data to different types of files. You will also study how to send and receive data over sockets.

## 8.1. Importing Files in Python

Before you work with any file in Python, you need to open the file. To do so, you can use the built-in open() function. You need to pass two attributes to the open() function: the path of the file to be opened and the mode in which you want to open a file.

The following table shows different types of mode values:

| Mode | Description |
|---|---|
| R | Opens file for read-only |
| r+ | Opens file for reading and writing |
| rb | Only Read file in binary |
| rb+ | Opens file to read and write in binary |
| w | Opens file to write only. Overwrites existing files with the same name |
| wb | Opens file to write only in binary. Overwrites existing files with the same name |
| w+ | Opens file for reading and writing |
| wb | Opens file to read and write in binary. Overwrites existing files with the same name |
| A | Opens a file for appending content at the end of the file |
| a+ | Opens file for appending as well as reading content |
| ab | Opens a file for appending content in binary |
| ab+ | Opens a file for reading and appending content in binary |

The following script opens a simple text file for reading and writing. The script also prints the object type returned by the open() function. Depending upon the file, the open() function returns an object which you can use to perform different types of operations on the file.

**Script 1:**

```
file_handle_text=open("E:/Datasets/my_text.txt","r+")
type(file_handle_text)
```

**Output:**

```
_io.TextIOWrapper
```

In the same way, you can open word files and pdf files as shown in scripts 2 and 3, respectively.

**Script 2:**

```
file_handle_word=open("E:/Datasets/my_text.docx","r+")
type(file_handle_word)
```

**Output:**

```
_io.TextIOWrapper
```

**Script 3:**

```
file_handle_pdf=open("E:/Datasets/my_text.pdf","r+")
type(file_handle_pdf)
```

**Output:**

```
_io.TextIOWrapper
```

You can print the complete file name along with the pathname, the file mode, and whether the file is closed or not using the name, mode, and closed attributes, respectively.

**Script 4:**

```
print(file_handle_pdf.name)
print(file_handle_pdf.mode)
print(file_handle_pdf.closed)
```

**Output:**

```
E:/Datasets/my_text.pdf
r+
False
```

Once you have opened a file, you must close it so that some other application can access it. To close a file, you need to call the closed() method.

**Script 5:**

```
file_handle_pdf.close()
print(file_handle_pdf.closed)
```

**Output:**

```
True
```

## 8.2. Working with Text Files

As the first example of reading and writing files with Python, you will see how to read and write text files with Python.

### 8.2.1. Reading Text Files

To read a text file with Python, you first have to open the file with read permissions and then call the read() method using the file handler object. The following script reads a file named "my_text.txt."

**Script 6:**

```
file_handle_text=open("E:/Datasets/my_text.txt","r+")
file_content=file_handle_text.read()
print(file_content)
```

The output shows that the file contains three lines of text. You can open your text file if you want.

**Output:**

```
hello there
Welcome to Python from zero to hero
You will learn Python in this book.
```

Instead of reading the whole file, you can also read a file partially. For instance, if you want to read a specific number of characters from a text file, you need to pass the number of characters as a parameter value to the read() function, as shown below:

**Script 7:**

```
file_handle_text=open("E:/Datasets/my_text.txt","r+")
file_content=file_handle_text.read(20)
print(file_content)
```

**Output:**

```
hello there
Welcome
```

Finally, you can also read a file line by line using the readline() function. The read line function is an iterator that returns the next line of text until all the lines have been read. Here is an example of the readline() function.

**Script 8:**

```
file_handle_text=open("E:/Datasets/my_text.txt","r+")
file_line1 =file_handle_text.readline()
file_line2 =file_handle_text.readline()
print(file_line1)
print(file_line2)
file_handle_text.close()
```

**Output:**

```
hello there

Welcome to Python from zero to hero
```

There is a special piece of code that lets you open a file, perform some operation and close the file without explicitly calling the close() function. The code starts with a keyword followed by the open function, the as keyword, and the file object name. Inside the with block, you can perform operation on the file using the file object name.

The following script opens the my_text.txt file in read mode. The file object is stored in the file_handle_text variable, which is then used to read all the file content.

**Script 9:**

```
withopen("E:/Datasets/my_text.txt", mode ='r')asfile_handle_
    text:
file_content=file_handle_text.read()
print(file_content)
```

**Output:**

```
hello there
Welcome to Python from zero to hero
You will learn Python in this book.
```

## 8.2.2. Writing/Creating Text Files

Before creating a text file, let's see how you can write text to an existing file. To do so, you need to open a file with the append mode 'a'. Next, to write text at the end of the existing text, you can call the write() method. The text to be written is passed as a parameter to the write() method. Here is an example:

**Script 10:**

```
file_handle_text=open("E:/Datasets/my_text.txt","a")
file_handle_text.write("This line is appended to the existing
    file")
file_handle_text.close()
```

Now, if you print the contents of the file my_text.txt, it will show the newly appended line in the output.

**Script 11:**

```
file_handle_text=open("E:/Datasets/my_text.txt","r+")
file_content=file_handle_text.read()
print(file_content)
```

**Output:**

```
hello there
Welcome to Python from zero to hero
You will learn Python in this book.This line is appended to
    the existing file
```

Finally, to create a new file, you need to call the open function with the file path and the 'w' mode. If the file with the same name doesn't exist, a new fill will be created. Else, if a file with the same name exists, the file contents will be overwritten.

**Script 12:**

```
file_handle_text=open("E:/Datasets/my_text2.txt","w")
file_handle_text.write("This line will overwrite the existing
    content or will be written in a new file")
file_handle_text.close()
```

## 8.3. Working with CSV Files

In this section, you will see how to read and write CSV files.

### 8.3.1. Reading CSV Files

To read a CSV file in Python, you first need to import the csv module. Next, you need to open the CSV file using the open() function. Next, you need to call the reader() function from the CSV module and pass it the file object. The reader() method returns a list that contains items that correspond to rows in the CSV file. You can then iterate through the list items. Here is an example.

**Script 13:**

```
import csv

with open("E:/Datasets/my_csvfile.csv", mode ='r')as file_
   handle_csv:
    file_content = csv.reader(file_handle_csv)
    for row in file_content:
        print(row)
```

**Output:**

```
['name', ' age', ' gender', ' city']
['jon', ' 25', ' male', ' london']
['ned', ' 30', ' male', ' paris']
['sara', '29', ' female', ' tokyo']
['elis', '20', ' female', ' toronto']
```

### 8.3.2. Writing CSV Files

To write a CSV file, you need to first create a list whose items correspond to the columns headers of the CSV file. For records, you need to create a list of lists where each internal list corresponds to CSV rows and items correspond to column values. After that, you need to open a CSV file with write mode. The file object is then passed to the write() method from the CSV module. The write() method returns the writer object. Finally, to write the header, pass the header list to the writerow() function. Similarly, to write rows, pass the records list to the writerows() method, as shown in the following script.

**Script 14:**

```
import csv

headers = ['Name', 'Age', 'Gender', 'City']

records = [ ['nick', 29, 'male', 'lyon'],
```

```
        ['joseph', 30, 'male', 'manchester'],
        ['zita', 35, 'female', 'berlin']]

with open("E:/Datasets/my_csvfile2.csv", mode ='w', newline =
    '')as file_handle_csv:
    csv_writer = csv.writer(file_handle_csv)
# writing the header
    csv_writer.writerow(headers)

# writing the rows
    csv_writer.writerows(records)
```

Let's read your newly created CSV file to see if records have been correctly added to the file.

**Script 15:**

```
import csv

with open("E:/Datasets/my_csvfile2.csv", mode ='r')as file_
   handle_csv:
    file_content = csv.reader(file_handle_csv)
    for row in file_content:
        print(row)
```

You can see the file contents of your newly created CSV file.

**Output:**

```
['Name', 'Age', 'Gender', 'City']
['nick', '29', 'male', 'lyon']
['joseph', '30', 'male', 'manchester']
['zita', '35', 'female', 'berlin']
```

## 8.4. Working with PDF Files

In this section, you will see how to read and write PDF files with Python. To read PDF files, you need to install the PyPDF2 module. You can do so with the following pip command.

```
#$ pip install PyPDF2
```

## 8.4.1. Reading PDF Files

To read a PDF file, you need to first open a file with the read binary mode. Next, you need to pass the file object to the PdfFileReader() method from the PyPDF2 module. The object returned by the PdfFileReader()method can then be used to read PDF files.

You can use the numPages attribute to get the number of pages in your PDF document, as shown below:

**Script 16:**

```
import PyPDF2
file_handle_pdf=open("E:/Datasets/my_text.pdf","rb")
pdf_object= PyPDF2.PdfFileReader(file_handle_pdf)
print(pdf_object.numPages)
```

**Output:**

```
3
```

To print the text, you first need to get the page using the getPage() method. Next, using the page object, you can call the extractText() method to get the page text. The following script prints the text of the first page in your PDF document.

**Script 17:**

```
page_one=pdf_object.getPage(0)
print(page_one.extractText())
```

```
hello there. This is a pdf file

You can read this file with Python

You can also write a PDF file with Python
```

To print the text from all the pages, you can simply iterate through all the pages, grab the current page using the getPage method, and print its text using the extractText() function. The following script prints text from all the pages in your PDF document.

**Script 18:**

```
for i in range(pdf_object.numPages):
    new_page = pdf_object.getPage(i)
    print("==================")
    print(new_page.extractText())
```

## 8.4.2. Writing PDF Files

Writing a PDF document with Python is a little complex. You cannot just add any text string directly to a PDF document due to format constraints. One way to write a PDF document is to get text from a particular page of a PDF document and then add that text to a new PDF document.

The following script creates an object of the PdfFileWriter class. This object will be used to write text to a PDF document.

Next, you get the first page of the my_text.pdf class. To add or write a page using the PDF writer object, you need to pass the page to the addPage() method of the writer.

The next step is to open the file that you want to write using the open() function. Finally, the file object returned by the open() function is passed to the write() method of the PDF writer object.

Here is an example. The following script reads the first page from the my_text.pdf file and adds that page to a newly created my_text2.pdf file.

**Script 19:**

```
pdf_writer= PyPDF2.PdfFileWriter()

## getting first page of my_text.pdf
file_handle_pdf=open("E:/Datasets/my_text.pdf","rb")
pdf_object= PyPDF2.PdfFileReader(file_handle_pdf)
page_one=pdf_object.getPage(0)

## adding first page to the pdf writer
pdf_writer.addPage(page_one)

## creating new pdf document
new_pdf_file=open("E:/Datasets/my_text2.pdf",'wb')

## saving new pdf file
pdf_writer.write(new_pdf_file)

## closing the file
new_pdf_file.close()
```

## 8.5. Sending and Receiving Data Over Sockets

To send and receive data from an application on the same or another computer, you can use sockets. A socket refers to a path signified by the combination of IP address and port number.

You can send or receive data over sockets using a Python script. In this section, you will see how to send and receive data over sockets. You will create two applications: server and client. The server application will listen to the client requests on a specific IP and will send data to a client whenever the client connects to the server.

### 8.5.1. Sending Data Through Sockets

To create a server, you need to create an object of the Socket class from the socket module.

Next, you need to bind the socket to a port. Binding a socket to a port means that the socket will send and receive data through that port. To bind a socket to a port, you need to call the bind() method. The first parameter is the IP address of the system from which you want to receive requests. If you pass an empty string as a first parameter, the system will serve requests from any other IP. The second parameter is the port that you want to bind your socket to.

Next, you need to call the listen() method using the Socket class object. The listen method specifies the number of connections to the queue. In the following script, five connections will be queued at a time, after which the new connections will not be accepted by the socket.

Finally, you need to call the accept() method on the socket object inside a loop. Calling accepts() method inside a loop will put the socket into a constant listening mode. Whenever a client tries to connect to the server, the accept() method will return the client connection and address.

To send data back to the client, you need to call the send() method on the connection and pass the data that you want to send to the client as the method parameter.

**Script 20:**

```
import socket

new_socket = socket.socket()
print("Socket successfully created")
```

```
port =5555

new_socket.bind(('', port))
print("socket connected to port %s" %(port))


new_socket.listen(5)
print("Server is listening to request")

while True:

    conn, clt_address = new_socket.accept()
    print('Received connection request from', clt_address)

    conn.send(b'Welcome to the server')

conn.close()
```

When you run the above script, the server will start listening at port 5555.

**Output:**

```
Socket successfully created
socket connected to port 5555
Server is listening to request
```

### 8.5.2. Receiving Data Through a Socket

To receive data through sockets, you again need to create a Socket class object. Next, you need to call connect() method with the IP address and the port number of the server. Finally, to receive data from the server, you need to call the recv() method with the number of bytes of data to receive.

**Script 21:**

```
# this script should be run in a new application
# -*- coding: utf-8 -*-
"""
Created on Sat Apr  3 13:24:23 2021

@author: usman
"""
# Import socket module
import socket


client_socket=socket.socket()

port =5555


client_socket.connect(('127.0.0.1', port))

print(client_socket.recv(2048))

client_socket.close()
```

When you run the above script, you will receive a message from the server, as shown below.

**Output:**

```
b'Welcome to the server'
```

On the server side, you will see the IP address and port of the client application with a message that a connection was successfully received.

```
Socket successfully created
socket connected to port 5555
Server is listening to request
Received connection request from ('127.0.0.1', 63569)
```

**Further Readings - File Handling in Python**

To study more about file handling in Python, please check the official documentation. (https://bit.ly/3sQdGiy). Get used to searching and reading this documentation. It is a great resource of knowledge.

**Hands-on Time - Exercise**

Now, it is your turn. Follow the instructions in **the exercises below** to check your understanding of file handling and socket programming in Python. The answers to these questions are given at the end of the book.

# Exercise 8.1

**Question 1:**

The value of "w" for mode attribute in the open() function:

A. Opens a file for writing
B. Creates a new file if a file with the same name doesn't exist
C. Overwrites all the contents of an existing file
D. All of the above

**Question 2:**

Which method of the csv.write object is used for adding a single record to a CSV file?

A. addrows()
B. writerows()
C. appendrows()
D. insertrows()

**Question 3:**

What are the values of the parameters that you need to pass to the connect() method of the socket() to connect to a remote server application through a socket?

A. Server name and server ip name
B. Server ip address and port number
C. Server ip address, port number, and application name
D. Both A and C

## Exercise 8.2

Create a new text file. Write three lines of text in the text file. Read all the text from the file line by line using the `with` operator.

# 9

# Regular Expressions in Python

In this chapter, you will study regular expressions. You will see what regular expressions are, what constitutes a regular expression, what are n metacharacters, and what are some of the different types of regular expression functions.

## 9.1. What Is Regex?

Regular expressions are used to perform different types of operations on strings. A regular expression in Python consists of two parts: a pattern and a function. Regular expression patterns are used to search patterns within a string, whereas functions are used to perform operations on strings returned by the patterns.

To use a regular expression in Python, you need to import the re module. Let's take a look at a very simple example of a regular expression.

The following script creates a regular expression with the pattern "^p.*y$". This regular expression matches all the strings that start with the character p and end with the character y.

In the following script, the function used for regular expression is match(), which returns True if a string matches the pattern specified by the regular expression.

The first parameter to the match function is the pattern to search for, and the second parameter is the string that you want to search for the pattern.

**Script 1:**

```
import re

pattern = '^p.*y$'
string_list = ["pathology", "biology", "geography",
    "psychology", "mathematics"]

for str in string_list:
    result = re.match(pattern, str)
    if result:
        print(str)
```

**Output:**

```
pathology
psychology
```

## 9.2. Specifying Patterns Using Meta Characters

Meta characters are special characters that are used to define a regular expression pattern. In this section, you will see some of these patterns.

### 9.2.1. Square Brackets []

Square brackets are used when you want to search a string for multiple patterns. For instance, the pattern in the following script returns all the strings that contain letters a or b anywhere in a string.

**Script 2:**

```
import re

pattern = '.*[ab].*'
string_list = ["pathology", "nic", "jos", "biology",
    "geography", "psychology", "mathematics"]

for str in string_list:
    result = re.match(pattern, str)
    if result:
        print(str)
```

**Output:**

```
pathology
biology
geography
mathematics
```

### 9.2.2. Period (.)

A period is used to search for any character at a specific position. The following script searches for all the strings with five or more letters anywhere in a string.

**Script 3:**

```
import re

pattern = '.....'
string_list = ["pathology", "nic", "jos", "biology",
    "geography", "psychology", "mathematics"]

for str in string_list:
    result = re.match(pattern, str)
    if result:
        print(str)
```

**Output:**

```
pathology
biology
geography
psychology
mathematics
```

## 9.2.3. Carrot (^) and Dollar ($)

The carrot symbol searches the letter or string at the beginning of a string, whereas the dollar sign is used to search for a character or a string at the end of another string. For example, the regular expression in the following script returns all strings that start with the alphabet p, followed by any number of characters (.*) and ends with the alphabet y.

**Script 4:**

```
import re

pattern = '^p.*y$'
string_list = ["pathology", "biology", "geography",
   "psychology", "mathematics"]

for str in string_list:
    result = re.match(pattern, str)
    if result:
        print(str)
```

**Output:**

```
pathology
psychology
```

## 9.2.4. Plus (+) and Question Mark (+)

The plus sign is used to search for one or more occurrences of patterns to the left of the sign. For instance, the pattern

".*og+y" will search for all strings that end with y and that contain the letter o, followed by any number of letter g to the left of the ending letter y.

**Script 5:**

```
import re

pattern = '.*og+y'
string_list = ["pathology", "biology", "geography",
   "psychology", "mathematics"]

for str in string_list:
    result = re.match(pattern, str)
    if result:
        print(str)
```

**Output:**

```
pathology
biology
psychology
```

On the other hand, the question mark sign is used to search for one or more occurrences of patterns to the right of the sign.

**Script 6:**

```
import re

pattern = '.*at?h'
string_list = ["pathology", "biology", "geography",
   "psychology", "mathematics"]

for str in string_list:
    result = re.match(pattern, str)
    if result:
        print(str)
```

**Output:**

```
pathology
mathematics
```

## 9.2.5. Alteration (|) and Grouping ()

Alteration sign (|) is used to specify an OR condition between two or more regular expression patterns. The grouping sign () is used to group two or more patterns. For instance, the pattern "(^p) | (.*s$)" matches all strings that start with either the letter p or end with the letter s. Here is an example.

**Script 7:**

```
import re

pattern = '(^p)|(.*s$)'
string_list = ["pathology", "biology", "geography",
   "psychology", "mathematics"]

for str in string_list:
    result = re.match(pattern, str)
    if result:
        print(str)
```

**Output:**

```
pathology
psychology
mathematics
```

## 9.2.6. Backslash

Backslash escapes special characters, which are normally used as meta characters in patterns. For instance, if you want to search for a dot symbol inside a string, you can do so via \. Expression. For instance, the pattern in the following script returns all the strings that start with "25."

**Script 8:**

```
import re

pattern = '25\.+.*'
string_list = ["pathology", "biology", "25.245", ""
    "geography", "psychology", "mathematics"]

for str in string_list:
    result = re.match(pattern, str)
    if result:
        print(str)
```

**Output:**

```
25.245
```

## 9.2.7. Special Sequences

Python regular expressions also contain some special sequences. For instance, the \A pattern searches for a string at the start. For example, the following script will match strings that start with *pat*.

**Script 9:**

```
import re

pattern = '\Apat'
string_list = ["pathology", "biology", "25.245", ""
    "geography", "psychology", "mathematics"]

for str in string_list:
    result = re.match(pattern,str)
    if result:
        print(str)
```

**Output:**

```
pathology
```

The \d+ operator searches for all the digits within a string. Here is an example.

**Script 10:**

```
import re

pattern ='\d+'
str="This is 10, he is 20"
result =re.findall(pattern,str)
print(result)
```

**Output:**

```
['10', '20']
```

The \D+ sequence, with a capital D, returns all the words in a string, except digits. Look at the following example.

**Script 11:**

```
import re

pattern ='\D+'
str="This is 10, he is 20"
result =re.findall(pattern,str)
print(result)
```

**Output:**

```
['This is ', ', he is ']
```

The \w+ sequence returns all the words except special characters within a string.

**Script 12:**

```
import re

pattern ='\w+'
str="This is % 10 # he is 20"
result =re.findall(pattern,str)
print(result)
```

**Output:**

```
['This', 'is', '10', 'he', 'is', '20']
```

The \W+ with a capital W returns only the special characters from within a string.

**Script 13:**

```
import re

pattern ='\W+'
str="This is % 10 # he is 20"
result =re.findall(pattern,str)
print(result)
```

**Output:**

```
[' ', ' % ', ' # ', ' ', ' ']
```

## 9.3. Regular Expression Functions in Python

In this section, you will see some of the most common regular expression functions. You have already seen the match() function in action. We will discuss the rest of the functions in this section.

### 9.3.1. The findall() function

The findall() function matches and returns all the words in a string that match a specific pattern.

**Script 14:**

```
import re

pattern ='\d+'
str="This is 10 he is 20 and the gate is 80"
result =re.findall(pattern,str)
print(result)
```

**Output:**

```
['10', '20', '80']
```

## 9.3.2. The split() function

The split() function splits a string at places where a match with the regular expression is found. For instance, the regular expression in the following script splits a string where a digit is encountered.

**Script 15:**

```
import re

pattern ='\d+'
str="This is 10 he is 20 and the gate is 80."
result =re.split(pattern,str)
print(result)
```

**Output:**

```
['This is ', ' he is ', ' and the gate is ', '.']
```

## 9.3.3. The sub() and the subn() functions

The sub() function substitutes a string with another string at places that match the specified pattern. For instance, the following script replaces all the digits in a string with the string XX.

**Script 16:**

```
import re

pattern ='\d+'
str="This is 10 he is 20 and the gate is 80."
new_str=re.sub(pattern,'XX',str)
print(new_str)
```

**Output:**

```
This is XX he is XX and the gate is XX.
```

The subn() function is quite similar to the sub() function. However, in addition to the updated string, the subn() function also returns the number of substitutions made.

For instance, in the following script, the subn() function makes three substitutions, as shown by the output.

**Script 17:**

```
import re

pattern ='\d+'
str="This is 10 he is 20 and the gate is 80."
new_str=re.subn(pattern,'XX',str)
print(new_str)
```

**Output:**

```
('This is XX he is XX and the gate is XX.', 3)
```

### 9.3.4. The search()

The search() method searches for a pattern within a string and returns the value and indexes of the first matched pattern. For instance, the following script searches for digits within a string. Since the first digit is 10, its value, i.e., 10, and its indexes (8–10) are returned.

**Script 18:**

```
import re

pattern ='\d+'
str="This is 10 he is 20 and the gate is 80."
result =re.search(pattern,str)
print(result)
```

**Output:**

```
<re.Match object; span=(8, 10), match='10'>
```

**Further Readings - Regular Expressions**

To study more about regular expressions in Python, please check the official documentation (https://bit.ly/3dQh8FB). Get used to searching and reading this documentation. It is a great resource of knowledge.

**Hands-on Time - Exercise**

Now, it is your turn. Follow the instructions in **the exercises below** to check your understanding of Regular Expressions in Python. The answers to these questions are given at the end of the book.

# Exercise 9.1

**Question 1:**

The pattern '(\Ag)|(\d+)' matches

A. All the digits

B. The strings with characters Ag

C. Strings that start with g or which are digits

D. All of the above

**Question 2:**

In Python, the function used to replace a string with another string is:

A. replace()

B. sub()

C. substitute()

D. rep()

**Question 3:**

The escape character used to escape meta characters within a regex pattern is:

A. Forward slash

B. Backslash

C. Alteration

D. Escape

## Exercise 9.2

Write a regular expression that returns all words from a list that contain a carrot (^) symbol or a dollar sign ($), or a plus (+) sign.

# 10

# Some Useful Python Modules

In the previous chapters, you studied some of the most fundamental Python concepts. In this chapter, you will study some very useful Python modules.

A Python module offers a collection of similar functionalities. For instance, the Python Math module allows you to perform various mathematical operations. Similarly, the DateTime module provides functions and objects that can be used to perform various operations related to date and time.

In this chapter, you will see how to use the following Python modules:

1. Debugger Module
2. Collections Module
3. DateTime Module
4. Math Module
5. Random Module
6. Time and Timeit Modules

## 10.1. Python Debugger

The debugger module, as the name suggests, is used to debug Python applications. If you want to know what value is being assigned to a variable at runtime, you can simply print the value on the console. However, if you want to check the value of multiple variables at runtime, you will have to print multiple statements at different locations in your code, which can clutter the code and can also affect the application's performance. This is where the Python debugger module comes into play.

The Python debugger module allows you to check the values of different variables at runtime. Let's see an example of how to use a Python debugger.

Let's write a simple script where we define a dictionary that contains some dummy item names and total sale prices for items. Next, we define a list that contains quantities for each item in the dictionary.

For instance, in the following script, the total price for the first item, i.e., laptop in the total_price dictionary, is 5, as can be seen from the first item in the quantities list.

Next, you execute a loop that displays item names and the average prices for all the items. The average price of an item in the total_price dictionary can be calculated by dividing the dictionary value for the item by the corresponding value in the quantity list.

For instance, the average price of the first item, i.e., laptop, can be calculated by dividing 100 by the first item in the quantity list, i.e., 5.

Execute the following script.

**Script 1:**

```
total_price = {'laptop': 100, 'cell phone': 75, 'keyboard':
   40, 'mic': 40, 'mouse': 15}

quantities = [5, 5, 5, 10, 5]

for (item, price), quantity in zip(total_price.items(),
   quantities):

    average_price = (price/quantity)
    print("The average price for a", item, "is", str(average_
   price))
```

**Output:**

```
The average price for a laptop is 20.0
The average price for a cell phone is 15.0
The average price for a keyboard is 8.0
The average price for a mic is 4.0
The average price for a mouse is 3.0
```

Now let's suppose that the quantity of one of the items is 0. If you run the following script, an exception will be thrown.

**Script 2:**

```
total_price = {'laptop': 100, 'cell phone': 75, 'keyboard':
   40, 'mic': 40, 'mouse': 15}

quantities = [5, 5, 0, 10, 5]

for (item, price), quantity in zip(total_price.items(),
   quantities):

    average_price = (price/quantity)
    print("The average price for a", item, "is", str(average_
   price))
```

The exception below is thrown because the value of the third item in the quantity list, which corresponds to the quantity of the keyboard, is 0. Hence, when the total price for all the keyboards, i.e., 40, is divided by 0, an exception is thrown.

**Output:**

```
The average price for a laptop is 20.0
The average price for a cell phone is 15.0
---------------------------------------------------------------
ZeroDivisionError                  Traceback (most recent call last)
<ipython-input-2-ee9c9bedee80> in <module>
      5for(item, price), quantity in zip(total_price.
   items(),quantities):
      6
----> 7average_price=(price/quantity)
      8      print("The average price for a", item,"is",
   str(average_price))

ZeroDivisionError: division by zero
```

Imagine a scenario where you are reading data from a list of thousand records. In this case, it is difficult to find the item for which the quantity is 0 by simply looking at the list. Another option is to print the item before printing its average price, as shown in the following script.

**Script 3:**

```
total_price = {'laptop': 100, 'cell phone': 75, 'keyboard':
   40, 'mic': 40, 'mouse': 15}

quantities = [5, 5, 0, 10, 5]

for (item, price), quantity in zip(total_price.items(),
   quantities):

    print(item)
    average_price = (price/quantity)
    print("The average price for a", item, "is", str(average_
   price))
```

From the output, you can see that the error occurs while printing the average price for the item keyboard.

**Output:**

```
laptop
The average price for a laptop is 20.0
cell phone
The average price for a cell phone is 15.0
keyboard
---------------------------------------------------------------
ZeroDivisionError              Traceback (most recent call last)
<ipython-input-3-3e1b22b4964b> in <module>
      6
      7     print(item)
----> 8average_price=(price/quantity)
      9     print("The average price for a", item,"is",
   str(average_price))

ZeroDivisionError: division by zero
```

However, if you have thousands of records, you will have to execute thousands of print statements for one variable. If you also want to print the value of the quantity variable, you will have to write another print statement or concatenate the value with the value of the item. Hence, a lot of computations will take place.

This is where the Python debugger comes to play. With the Python debugger, you can keep track of all the variables in your application.

To debug an application with the Python debugger, you need to import the pdb module. Next, you need to call the method set_trace() at that point in the code where you want to check the values of the variable defined by the set_trace() method. Once the code hits that point, a text field will be displayed where you can check the value of a variable by typing the variable name.

In the following script, you wrap the code that is likely to throw an exception in a try block. Since the exception will be caught in the except block, you call the pdb.set_trace() method in the exception block. Run the following script to see this in action.

**Script 4:**

```
import pdb

total_price = {'laptop': 100, 'cell phone': 75, 'keyboard':
   40, 'mic': 40, 'mouse': 15}

quantities = [5, 5, 0, 10, 5]

for (item, price), quantity in zip(total_price.items(),
   quantities):

    try:
        average_price = (price/quantity)
        print("The average price for a", item, "is",
   str(average_price))
    except:
        pdb.set_trace()
```

Since the above code will throw an exception that will be caught in the except block, the call to set_trace() method will execute, and you will see a text field appear in the output, as shown below.

Type the name of a variable in the text box to see its value. For instance, if you type an item, you will see "keyboard" in the output, as shown below.

**Output:**

```
ipdb> item

The average price for a laptop is 20.0
The average price for a cell phone is 15.0
> <ipython-input-4-8568c88c1e27>(7)<module>()
      5 quantities = [5, 5, 0, 10, 5]
      6
----> 7 for (item, price), quantity in zip(total_price.items(),quantities):
      8
      9     try:
```

```
The average price for a laptop is 20.0
The average price for a cell phone is 15.0
> <ipython-input-4-8568c88c1e27>(7)<module>()
      5 quantities = [5, 5, 0, 10, 5]
      6
----> 7 for (item, price), quantity in zip(total_price.items(),quantities):
      8
      9     try:

ipdb> item
'keyboard'

ipdb>
```

Similarly, you can type *price* and *quantity* in the text field to see their values. See how simple it is? You don't have to execute any print statement; your code will remain clean, and yet you will be able to check the values of all the variables in your code.

Finally, to quit the Python debugger, simply type the letter *q* and hit enter.

## 10.2. Collections Module

In addition to basic collections like lists, tuples, and dictionaries, Python offers some advanced collections in the collection's module. These collections are used to perform special functions, such as counting the total number of items in a list, etc. In this section, you will see some of the most commonly used collections.

### 10.2.1. Counters

A Counter is a type of collection that can be used to count the occurrence of each item in a list. Let's see this with the help of an example.

The following script imports the Counter class from the collection's module.

**Script 5:**

```
from collections import Counter
```

Next, we create a list of different car manufacturers. To create an object of a Counter class, you can pass a list to the Counter. The following script creates a Counter class using the cars list. The Counter is printed on the console.

**Script 6:**

```
cars =["Honda","Honda","Honda","Honda","Ford","Ford",
    "BMW","BMW","BMW","BMW","BMW","BMW","BMW"]

print(Counter(cars))
```

In the output below, you can see the count of each item in the cars list. For instance, you can see that the item BMW exists for seven times in the cars list and so on.

**Output:**

```
Counter({'BMW': 7, 'Honda': 4, 'Ford': 2})
```

A Counter is a type of dictionary. To access the count of any individual item, you can pass the item name as an index value to the Counter. For instance, the following script prints the count for the item *Honda*.

**Script 7:**

```
cars_count= Counter(cars)
print(cars_count["Honda"])
```

**Output:**

```
4
```

Since a string is essentially a list of characters, you can create a Counter object using a string. Such a Counter will contain the count for each character in the string. Look at the following example for reference.

**Script 8:**

```
str_count= Counter("adklasjdkasdlaj")
print(str_count)
```

**Output:**

```
Counter({'a': 4, 'd': 3, 'k': 2, 'l': 2, 's': 2, 'j': 2})
```

### 10.2.2. Default Dictionaries

Default dictionary is a type of collection similar to an ordinary dictionary. However, in a default dictionary, you can specify a default value for keys that don't exist in the dictionary.

Let's see the difference between a normal dictionary and a default dictionary.

The following script creates a dictionary normal_dic with the names of cars and their counts. Since the item *BMW* exists in the normal_dic, its value will be printed on the console.

**Script 9:**

```
from collections importdefaultdict

normal_dic={'BMW':7,'Honda':4,'Ford':2}
print(normal_dic["BMW"])
```

**Output:**

```
7
```

Now let's try to access a dictionary item with a key that doesn't exist.

**Script 10:**

```
print(normal_dic["Toyota"])
```

Since the item with the key *Toyota* doesn't exist in the normal_dic dictionary, you will see the following exception.

**Output:**

```
---------------------------------------------------------------
KeyError                          Traceback (most recent call last)
<ipython-input-175-800fb535cdac> in <module>
----> 1print(normal_dic["Toyota"])

KeyError: 'Toyota'
```

With default dictionaries, you can assign a default value to a dictionary. To create a default dictionary, you can use the keyword defaultdic. In the constructor, you need to pass a lambda expression with a value that you want to return in case if a key is not found in a dictionary. In the following script, you pass the string *Not Available* for keys that are not present in a dictionary.

Next, you pass the keys *BMW* and *Toyota* to your default dictionary named def_dic. Since the key *BMW* exists in the dictionary, you will see its corresponding value, i.e., 7. For the key *Toyota*, the string *Not Available* will be printed, and no exception will be thrown.

**Script 11:**

```
from collections import defaultdict

def_dic = defaultdict(lambda: "Not Available")
def_dic["BMW"] = 7

print(def_dic["BMW"])
print(def_dic["Toyota"])
```

**Output:**

```
7
Not Available
```

### 10.2.3. Named Tuples

The named tuple is a type of tuple with named indexes.

In the case of a normal tuple, you can access items by zero-based indexes. For instance, to access the first item in a tuple, you can pass 0 as the index value. In the case of a named tuple, you can access a tuple element by passing a named value, i.e., string, etc., as a tuple index.

Let's see the difference between a named tuple and a normal tuple.

The following script creates a normal tuple with three elements. The third element is printed on the console by passing 2 as the index value for the tuple.

**Script 12:**

```
normal_tuple=("BMW",10,"Black")
print(normal_tuple[2])
```

**Output:**

```
Black
```

Let's now see an example of a named tuple. To create a named tuple, you can use the namedtuple class from the collections module. In the construction, you need to pass the identifier for the named tuple, followed by a list of index names.

For instance, in the following script, you create a name tuple *car_tuple* object with the identifier name Car. Next, you create a list with three index names *Name*, *Model*, and *Color*.

Now, if you create an object of this named tuple, you need to pass values for the *Name*, *Model*, and *Color* indexes, as you can see in the following script.

**Script 13:**

```
from collections import namedtuple

car_tuple = namedtuple('Car', ['Name', 'Model', 'Color'])
cars = car_tuple(Name = "BMW", Model=10, Color = "Black")
```

Now, you can assess the items in the named tuple object *cars* using the index names. For instance, to access the third item, you can either use the integer index 2 or the named index *Color,* as shown in the following script.

**Script 14:**

```
print(cars[2])
print(cars.Color)
```

**Output:**

```
Black
Black
```

## 10.3. DateTime Module

The DateTime module in Python is used to store data of type date and time. With the DateTime module, you can create objects, which can then be used to access date-time information such as year, months, days, hours, minutes, and seconds.

Let's see an example. The following script returns a datetime object, which contains the current date and time of your system using the now() method from the datetime class of the datetime module.

The current time is then printed on the console. To display the current time in a string format, you need to call the ctime() method on your datetime object.

**Script 15:**

```
import datetime

datetime_now=datetime.datetime.now()

print(datetime_now)
print(datetime_now.ctime())
```

**Output:**

```
2021-04-11 10:37:45.726437
Sun Apr 11 10:37:45 2021
```

To see all the attributes of the datetime class, you can pass the datetime object that was created in the last script to the dir() method, as shown below.

**Script 16:**

```
print(dir(datetime_now))
```

**Output:**

```
['__add__',
'__class__',
'__delattr__',
'__dir__',
'__doc__',
'__eq__',
'__format__',
'__ge__',
'__getattribute__',
'__gt__',
'__hash__',
'__init__',
'__init_subclass__',
'__le__',
'__lt__',
'__ne__',
'__new__',
'__radd__',
'__reduce__',
'__reduce_ex__',
'__repr__',
'__rsub__',
'__setattr__',
'__sizeof__',
'__str__',
'__sub__',
'__subclasshook__',
'astimezone',
'combine',
'ctime',
'date',
'day',
'dst',
'fold',
'fromisocalendar',
'fromisoformat',
'fromordinal',
'fromtimestamp',
```

```
'hour',
'isocalendar',
'isoformat',
'isoweekday',
'max',
'microsecond',
'min',
'minute',
'month',
'now',
'replace',
'resolution',
'second',
'strftime',
'strptime',
'time',
'timestamp',
'timetuple',
'timetz',
'today',
'toordinal',
'tzinfo',
'tzname',
'utcfromtimestamp',
'utcnow',
'utcoffset',
'utctimetuple',
'weekday',
'year']
```

From the output, you can see that the datetime object can be used to store various information about a date such as year, weekday, second, timestamp, minute, hour, microsecond, etc.

Let's now try to find the number of seconds between two dates. To do so, you have to subtract one datetime object from the other. Next, on the object returned as a result of subtraction, call the total_seconds() methods, as shown below:

**Script 17:**

```
date1 =datetime.datetime.now()
date2 =datetime.datetime(1990,4,10)

date_dif= date1-date2
print(date_dif.days)
print(date_dif.total_seconds())
```

**Output:**

```
11324
978431869.338581
```

You can simply divide the number of seconds by 3,600 to get the total number of hours. And to get the total number of days, divide the number of seconds by 86,400.

### 10.3.1. Working with Time Only

You can work with time exclusively using the time object of the datetime module. The following script creates a new time object and then prints the object type and its attributes and methods.

**Script 18:**

```
import datetime

new_time=datetime.time()

print(type(new_time))
print(dir(new_time))
```

**Output:**

```
<class 'datetime.time'>

['__class__', '__delattr__', '__dir__', '__doc__', '__eq__',
    '__format__', '__ge__', '__getattribute__', '__gt__',
    '__hash__', '__init__', '__init_subclass__', '__le__', '__
    lt__', '__ne__', '__new__', '__reduce__', '__reduce_ex__',
    '__repr__', '__setattr__', '__sizeof__', '__str__', '__
    subclasshook__', 'dst', 'fold', 'fromisoformat', 'hour',
    'isoformat', 'max', 'microsecond', 'min', 'minute',
    'replace', 'resolution', 'second', 'strftime', 'tzinfo',
    'tzname', 'utcoffset']
```

The following script creates a time object with a time value of 5 hours and 30 minutes. Next, the values of hour, minute, seconds, and microsecond attributes, are displayed.

**Script 19:**

```
new_time=datetime.time(5,30)
print(new_time.hour)
print(new_time.minute)
print(new_time.second)
print(new_time.microsecond)
```

Since you did not specify any value for second and microsecond attributes, you can see 0 in the output for these attributes.

**Output:**

```
5
30
0
0
```

You can also replace the value of the hour, minute, or second using the replace() function.

The following script uses the replace() function to replace the value of an hour in a time object.

**Script 20:**

```
new_time=new_time.replace(hour =7)
print(new_time.hour)
```

**Output:**

```
7
```

### 10.3.2. Working Dates Only

You can also create objects that store information about the date only (no time information), as shown in the following script.

**Script 21:**

```
import datetime

new_date=datetime.date(2019,2,10)

print(new_date.ctime())
```

**Output:**

```
Sun Feb 10 00:00:00 2019
```

The following script prints the attributes and functions of the date object.

**Script 22:**

```
print(dir(new_date))
```

**Output:**

```
['__add__', '__class__', '__delattr__', '__dir__', '__doc__',
   '__eq__', '__format__', '__ge__', '__getattribute__',
   '__gt__', '__hash__', '__init__', '__init_subclass__',
   '__le__', '__lt__', '__ne__', '__new__', '__radd__',
   '__reduce__', '__reduce_ex__', '__repr__', '__rsub__',
   '__setattr__', '__sizeof__', '__str__', '__sub__',
   '__subclasshook__', 'ctime', 'day', 'fromisocalendar',
   'fromisoformat', 'fromordinal', 'fromtimestamp',
   'isocalendar', 'isoformat', 'isoweekday', 'max', 'min',
   'month', 'replace', 'resolution', 'strftime', 'timetuple',
   'today', 'toordinal', 'weekday', 'year']
```

Finally, you can also replace day, month, and other attributes in a date object using the replace() function.

The following script replaces the day of a date object.

**Script 23:**

```
import datetime

new_date=datetime.date(2019,2,10)
new_date=new_date.replace(day =20)
print(new_date.ctime())
```

**Output:**

```
Wed Feb 20 00:00:00 2019
```

## 10.4. Math Module

The Math module in Python is used to perform different types of mathematical operations.

The following script converts an angle from degrees to radians using the radians() function.

**Script 24:**

```
import math

angle =math.radians(90)
print(angle)
```

**Output:**

```
1.5707963267948966
```

The following script finds the sine, cosine, and tangent values of an angle. The angle value is passed in radians to the sin(), cos(), and tan() functions, respectively.

**Script 25:**

```
print(math.sin(angle))
print(math.cos(angle))
print(math.tan(angle))
```

**Output:**

```
1.0
6.123233995736766e-17
1.633123935319537e+16
```

You can use the pow() method from the Math module to raise an integer to the power of another integer. For instance, the following script prints the result when the integer 4 is raised to the power of 5.

**Script 26:**

```
print(math.pow(4,5))
```

**Output:**

```
1024.0
```

Similarly, you can find the square root of an integer using the sqrt() method, as shown below.

**Script 27:**

```
print(math.sqrt(225))
```

**Output:**

```
15.0
```

You can also calculate natural log and log with the base 10, using the log() and log10() functions, as shown in the following script:

**Script 28:**

```
print(math.log(100))
print(math.log10(100))
```

**Output:**

```
4.605170185988092
2.0
```

## 10.5. Random Module

The Random module in Python is used to perform operations like random number generation and selecting random values from a list.

To generate a random number between 0 and 1, simply call the random() function from the random module, as shown in the following script.

**Script 29:**

```
import random

print(random.random())
```

**Output:**

```
0.6631112113673787
```

To generate a random integer within a particular range, you can use the randint() function. You need to pass the lower bound and upper bound as parameter values.

For instance, the following script generates three random integers between 0 and 50.

**Script 30:**

```
print(random.randint(0,50))
print(random.randint(0,50))
print(random.randint(0,50))
```

**Output:**

```
31
2
17
```

You can also use the randrange() function to generate a random integer between a range of two values. However, with the randrange() function, you can also specify the step for the generation of a random integer.

For instance, in the following script, the randrange() function first generates any random integer between 0 and 1. In the second line, a random number, which is a multiple of 3, is generated using the randrange() function. Finally, a random integer, which is a multiple of 5, is generated.

**Script 31:**

```
print(random.randrange(0,50))
print(random.randrange(0,50,3))
print(random.randrange(0,50,5))
```

**Output:**

```
27
27
20
```

You can also select an item from a list randomly using the choice() function from the random module. Here is an example:

**Script 32:**

```
cars =[1,15,36,14,15,10]
print(random.choice(cars))
```

**Output:**

```
14
```

Finally, to randomly shuffle items within a list, you can use the shuffle() function from the Random module. Take a look at the following example:

**Script 33:**

```
cars =[1,15,36,14,15,10]
cars_shuffle=random.shuffle(cars)
print(cars_shuffle)
```

**Output:**

```
None
```

## 10.6. Find Execution time of Python Scripts

Execution time is an important metric for measuring the performance of a specific piece of code. In programming, you can implement the same logic using different pieces of code. However, you should select an approach that is not very slow. Otherwise, users will have to wait for long periods to perform desired tasks using your application.

In Python, there are three main ways to find the execution time of a script. You can use time and time modules. If you are using the Jupyter Notebook, you can also use the ##timeit command to find the execution time of a script.

Let's write two programs that calculate the value of the Fibonacci number. The first program will use a recursive function, while the second program will use simple *for* loops. We will then compare the execution time of both the programs using different approaches in Python.

The following script defines a method named get_fib(), which calculates the value of a Fibonacci number using a recursive function.

**Script 34:**

```
def get_fib(num):
    if num == 1 or num == 2:
        return 1
    else:
        return get_fib(num-1) + get_fib(num-2)

get_fib(20)
```

**Output:**

```
6765
```

The following script defines the get_fib2() method, which calculates the value of a Fibonacci number using a for loop.

**Script 35:**

```
def get_fib2(num):


    if num == 1:
        return 0

    if num == 2:
        return 1

    num1 = 1
    num2 = 1
```

```
    for i in range(3, num+1):

        val = num1 + num2

        num1 = num2
        num2 = val
    return val

get_fib2(20)
```

**Output:**

```
6765
```

## 10.6.1. Using Time Module

The time module in Python can calculate the execution time of a Python script. To do so, you need to call the time() method before and after the script for which you want to measure the execution time. Next, you simply subtract the timestamp before the execution of the script from the timestamp after the execution of the script.

The following script measures the execution time for the get_fib() function for calculating the 30th number in the Fibonacci series.

**Script 36:**

```
import time

start_time=time.time()

get_fib(30)

end_time=time.time()

script_time=end_time-start_time
print(str(script_time))
```

**Output:**

```
0.28528690338134766
```

Similarly, the following script calculates the execution time for the get_fib2() function for calculating the 30th number in the Fibonacci series.

**Script 37:**

```
import time

start_time=time.time()

val= get_fib2(30)
end_time=time.time()

script_time=end_time-start_time
print(str(script_time))
```

The output shows 0.0 because the value is too minute to be displayed.

**Output:**

```
0.0
```

The comparison shows that the get_feb2() function, which uses *for* loops, is faster than the get_feb() function, which uses a recursive function, for calculating the value of the 30th number in the Fibonacci series.

### 10.6.2. Using Timeit Module

You can also use the timeit module for calculating the execution time of a program. To do so, you need to call the timeit() method from the timeit module. You need to pass the function call and the function script that you want to measure for execution speed as string parameters to the timeit() method.

The following script stores the function call and the function body in the string format in the variables statement and setup, respectively.

**Script 38:**

```
statement = "get_fib(30)"

setup = """
def get_fib(num):
    if num == 1 or num == 2:
        return 1
    else:
        return get_fib(num-1) + get_fib(num-2)
"""
```

Next, while calling the timeit() method, you pass the statement variable (which contains the function call in string format) as the first parameter value and the setup variable (which contains the function script in string format) as the second parameter value. The third parameter, i.e., the number corresponds to the number of times the number of executions.

**Script 39:**

```
importtimeit
timeit.timeit(statement, setup, number =100)
```

The output shows that the get_feb() method took 37.98 seconds to calculate the 30th Fibonacci number 100 times.

**Output:**

```
37.98757040000055
```

Similarly, the following script uses the timeit module to measure the execution time of the get_fib2() method for calculating the 30th Fibonacci number 100 times.

**Script 40:**

```
statement = "get_fib2(30)"
setup = """
def get_fib2(num):


    if num == 1:
        return 0

    if num == 2:
        return 1

    num1 = 1
    num2 = 1

    for i in range(3, num+1):

        val = num1 + num2

        num1 = num2
        num2 = val
    return val
    """
```

**Script 41:**

```
importtimeit
timeit.timeit(statement, setup, number =100)
```

The get_feb2() only took 0.0004, seconds as shown below:

**Output:**

```
0.000453499998911866
```

The comparison shows that the get_feb2() function, which uses *for* loops, is again faster than the get_feb() function, which uses a recursive function, for calculating the value of the 30th number in the Fibonacci series.

### 10.6.3 The ##timeit Command

If you are using the Jupyter Notebook, you can find the execution time of a particular script by simply adding the command %%timeit command at the top of the cell that contains your script.

Run the following script in a Jupyter Notebook cell to find the execution time of the get_fib() method using the %%timeit module.

**Script 42:**

```
%%timeit
get_fib(30)
```

**Output:**

```
266 ms ± 6.48 ms per loop (mean ± std. dev. of 7 runs, 1 loop
   each)
```

Similarly, run the following script in a Jupyter Notebook cell to find the execution time of the get_fib2() method using the %%timeit module.

**Script 43:**

```
%%timeit
get_fib2(30)
```

**Output:**

```
2.55 µs ± 235 ns per loop (mean ± std. dev. of 7 runs, 100000
   loops each)
```

In this chapter, you have seen how to work with some of the most useful modules in Python. In the next chapter, you will see how to create your custom modules in Python.

**Further Readings - Collections and DateTime Module**

To study more about regular Python Collections module, check this link: https://bit.ly/3dSD9no
To study more about the DateTime Module, check this link: https://bit.ly/3tWCoz6

**Hands-on Time - Exercise**

Now, it is your turn. Follow the instructions in **the exercises below** to check your understanding of the Python modules discussed in this chapter. The answers to these questions are given at the end of the book.

# Exercise 10.1

**Question 1:**

Which command is used to close the Python debugger?

A. quit

B. close

C. q

D. c

**Question 2:**

The following expression is used to specify a default value to default dictionaries in Python.

A. defaultdictionary(lambda: "value")

B. defaultdict(lambda = "value")

C. DefaultDict(lambda : "value")

D. none of the above

**Question 3:**

Which of the following modules and expressions can be used to find script time in Jupyter?

A. ##

B. timeit

C. time

D. all of the above

## Exercise 10.2

Find the number of counts for each unique value in the following list using the *for* loop and the Counter object `[Apple, Orange, Apple, Apple, Orange, Banana, Orange, Orange]`.

# 11

# Creating Custom Modules in Python

In the previous chapter, you studied some of the Python modules to perform some routine tasks. In this chapter, you will study how you can create your own custom Python modules.

## 11.1. Why You Need Modules?

Before you study the process of module development in Python, it is important to understand why you need modules in the first place. The one-word answer to this question is reusability.

A module helps you implement functionality that you can use across multiple applications. For instance, you can develop a module that contains various functions for interaction with a database. You can use this module in multiple applications.

Another benefit of module development is flexible code management. With modules, you can divide your application into multiple files that are easier to manage as compared to one big file containing all the functionalities of an application.

Now that you know why modules can make your life easier, let's see how you can develop a module in Python.

## 11.2. Creating and Importing a Basic Module

A module is nothing more than a Python file. To create a module, you just need to create a Python file and add write the module functionalities to that file. Like any other Python file, a module can contain functions, attributes, classes, etc.

Let's create our first module. We will name it mymodule. To create a module named mymodule, you need to create a Python file named mymodule.py. Notice the extension*.py* here, which shows that a Python module is just another Python file.

Let's add a simple function named: show_message() to our module. This function prints a string on the console.

**Script 1:**

```
def show_message():
    print("Hello from your custom module")
```

And that's it. You have created a module named mymodule with one function, show_message().

To use this module in your Python application, you need to create another Python and save it in the same directory where you saved your module file mymodule.py.

You can give any name to the new file. I will name it test.py. To use the module mymodule in the file test.py, you need to import the mymodule first. You can import your custom module in the same way as you imported built-in Python modules in the last chapter. You have to use the keyword *import,* followed by the module name *mymodule*.

Remember, though the file name for the module is mymodule.py, you will not specify the*.py* extension while importing the module. You simply have to write the module name without an extension.

To access attributes, functions, or classes from a module, you can use the module name, followed by the dot operator and the attribute or function that you need to call.

The following script imports the module mymodule in the test.py file and calls its function show_message().

**Script 2:**

```
import mymodule

mymodule.show_message()
```

**Output:**

```
Hello from your custom module
```

In addition to using a dot operator to access a module function or attribute, you can directly import a module function, as well. To do so, you can use the import keyword. For instance, the following script imports the show_message() function from the mymodule module.

**Script 3:**

```
from mymodule import show_message

show_message()
```

**Output:**

```
Hello from your custom module
```

Let's now add another function, find_square(), to our mymodule module. The find_Square() function accepts a number and returns its square. Update the mymodule.py file with the following script.

**Script 4:**

```
def show_message():
    print("Hello from your custom module")

def find_square(num):
    return num * num
```

Now, you have two functions in your mymodule module. The following script imports the show_message() function from the mymodule module in the test.py file. Next, you call the find_square() function.

**Script 5:**

```
from mymodule import show_message

find_square(5s)
```

Here is the output of the above script. The output shows that the find_square function is not defined.

**Output:**

```
NameError: name 'find_square' is not defined
```

The reason behind this error is that in Script 5, the import function doesn't import everything from the mymodule module. It only imports the show_message() function. However, you called the find_square() function, which is not imported.

To import everything from a module, you need to add an asterisk after the import keyword.

The following script imports everything from the mymodule module in the test.py file.

Now, you can call both show_message() and find_square() functions in your test.py file, as shown below.

**Script 6:**

```
from mymodule import*

show_message()
result = find_square(5)
    print(result)
```

**Output:**

```
Hello from your custom module
25
```

## 11.3. Creating and Importing Multiple Modules

You can also create multiple custom modules and import them into your application. Also, one module can use functionalities from another module.

Let's create a module named mymodule2. To do so, create a file named mymodule2.py in the same directory as mymodule.py and your test file where you import modules, which is test.py in this case.

Add the following script to your mymodule2.py file. The mymodule2 imports your mymodule module, which you previously created.

The mymodule2 contains a function find_cube() which returns the cube of the number passed to it. Inside the find_cube() method, the number is passed to the find_square() method of the mymodule module.

The value returned by the find_square() method is then multiplied by the input number, which equates to the cube the input number.

### Script 7:

```
import mymodule

def find_cube(num):
    return num * mymodule.find_square(num)
```

In the test.py file, you can import the mymodule2 module and import everything from it, as shown in the following script. You can then calculate the cube of any number using the find_cube() function.

### Script 8:

```
from mymodule2 import *


result = find_cube(5)
    print(result)
```

### Output:

```
125
```

You can also import the mymodule and mymodule2 individually. The following script calculates the square of a number using the find_square() method of the mymodule module and finds the cube of a number using the find_cube() method of the mymodule2 module.

### Script 9:

```
import mymodule
import mymodule2

result = mymodule.find_square(5)
    print(result)

result = mymodule2.find_cube(5)
    print(result)
```

**Output:**

```
25
125
```

## 11.4. Adding Classes to Custom Modules

Just like functions, you can add classes to a module, as well. Let's see an example. You will create a simple class CustomClass inside the mymodule. To do so, update the mymodule.py file so that it contains the following script. Your CustomClass contains two methods: show_message() and find_square().

**Script 10:**

```
class CustomClass:

def show_message(self):
    print("Hello from your custom module")

def find_square(self, num):
    return num * num
```

You can now import the CustomClass from the mymodule in your application, as shown in the following script, which calls the find_square() method of the CustomClass.

**Script 11:**

```
import mymodule


my_class = mymodule.CustomClass()

result = my_class.find_square(5)
    print(result)
```

**Output:**

```
25
```

# 11.5. Importing Modules from a Different Path

In the previous section, you placed your module file and your test file in the same directory. However, you can also save your module file in a different directory and still import the module into your application. Let's see how you can do so.

Create a file named mymodule3.py. Add the following script to the file, and save it in a directory different than the directory of your text file.

**Script 12:**

```
class CustomClass3:

def show_message(self):
    print("Hello from your custom module")

def find_square(self, num):
    return num * num
```

Suppose you saved your mymodule3.py file in the directory *E:/modules*. Before you import the mymodule3 into your application, you need to include the *E:/modules* directory in the list of paths where your Python interpreter will search for modules. To do so, you can use the append() method from the path object of the sys module, as shown below:

**Script 13:**

```
import sys

sys.path.append("E:/modules")
```

Now, you can import any module that is inside the *E:/modules* directory in your application. For example, the following script imports the module mymodule3 and then calls the find_square() method of the CustomClass3 from the mymodule3 module.

**Script 14:**

```
import mymodule3


my_class3 = mymodule3.CustomClass3()

result = my_class3.find_square(5)
    print(result)
```

**Output:**

```
25
```

## 11.6. Adding Modules to Python Path

When you import a module, the Python interpreter searches the module in various Paths. To see all the paths accessible to the Python interpreter, you can use the following scripts.

**Script 15:**

```
import sys
print(sys.path)
```

The output will look something like this. Depending upon your Python installation directory and the packages you have installed, your output might look different.

**Output:**

```
['C:\\ProgramData\\Anaconda3\\python38.zip', 'C:\\
   ProgramData\\Anaconda3\\DLLs', 'C:\\ProgramData\\
   Anaconda3\\lib', 'C:\\ProgramData\\Anaconda3', '', 'C:\\
   ProgramData\\Anaconda3\\lib\\site-packages', 'C:\\
   ProgramData\\Anaconda3\\lib\\site-packages\\email-6.0.0a1-
   py3.8.egg', 'C:\\ProgramData\\Anaconda3\\lib\\site-
   packages\\win32', 'C:\\ProgramData\\Anaconda3\\lib\\site-
   packages\\win32\\lib', 'C:\\ProgramData\\Anaconda3\\lib\\
   site-packages\\Pythonwin',
```

To add your custom module to the default path for Python packages, look for the path which contains your site-packages. If you have installed Python via Anaconda, your path should look something like this.

C:\\ProgramData\\Anaconda3\\lib\\site-packages'

Save your mymodule3.py file in this path. Now, you can call functionalities from the mymodule3 module without explicitly adding the path of the mymodule3.py file into your application.

**Script 16:**

```
import mymodule3

my_class3 = mymodule3.CustomClass3()

result = my_class3.find_square(5)
    print(result)
```

**Output:**

```
25
```

**Further Readings - Python Modules**

To study more about Python modules, please check the official Python documentation (https://bit.ly/3tVIsZN). Get used to searching and reading this documentation. It is a great resource of knowledge.

**Hands-on Time - Exercise**

Now, it is your turn. Follow the instructions in **the exercises below** to check your understanding of custom modules in Python. The answers to these questions are given at the end of the book.

## Exercise 11.1

**Question 1:**

To create a custom module in Python, you need to create:

A. an object

B. a Python file

C. a class

D. a function

**Question 2:**

To create a class in a custom module, you need to:

A. add a keyword mymodule

B. add a keyword module

C. add a keyword module class

D. none of the above

**Question 3:**

In python, you can have __ levels for module dependencies:

A. unlimited

B. 1

C. 2

D. 3

## Exercise 11.2

Perform the following tasks:

Create a custom module1 that contains a function that returns the cube of a number.

Create a custom module2 that imports module 1 and contains a function that returns the sum of cubes of two numbers.

Import module1 and module2 and first find the cube of a number, and then find the sum of cubes of two numbers.

# 12

# Creating GUI in Python

Until now, you have been writing Python code that displays data in the console output. However, most modern Python applications will require you to develop graphical user interfaces (GUI). Various Python libraries allow you to develop GUI. However, Tkinter (https://docs.python.org/3/library/tkinter.html) is the only built-in Python library for GUI development.

In this chapter, you will see how to develop a basic GUI using the Python Tkinter library.

## 12.1. Creating a Basic Window

To create a simple window with Tkinter, you can use the Tk class from the Tkinter module, as shown in the script below. You need to call the mainloop() method on the object of the Tk class.

The mainloop() method keeps the window visible on the screen. Without the mainloop() method, the window will appear and immediately disappear.

Execute the following script to see how to create a basic window in Python.

**Script 1:**

```
# importing tkinter
from tkinter import *

# creating instance of Tk class
main_window = Tk()
type(main_window)

# displaying the main window
main_window.mainloop()
```

**Output:**

You can set the title of the window using the title attribute. Similarly, to set the window's width, height, and location, you can use the geometry attribute. The width and height in pixels and the distance in pixels from the top and left of the screen are specified in the following format: Width x Height + Distance from left + Distance from the top.

The following script sets the width and height of the window to 500 pixels. The distance from the left of the screen will be 100 pixels, while the distance from the top of the screen will be 200 pixels.

## Script 2:

```
# importing tkinter
from tkinter import *

# creating instance of Tk class
main_window = Tk()

# setting window title
main_window.title("Welcome to Python")

# setting window dimensions
main_window.geometry("500x500+100+200")

# displaying the main window
main_window.mainloop()
```

## Output:

Let's add a simple label to our window. To do so, you need to create an object of the Label class. In the constructor, the window name to which you want to attach the label is passed as the first parameter. The label text is passed to the text parameter, as shown below.

You also need to call the pack() method on the Label class object to attach the label to the window.

**Script 3:**

```
# importing tkinter
from tkinter import *

# creating instance of Tk class
main_window = Tk()

# creating the default label
my_label = Label(main_window, text = "Welcome to Python")

# attaching default label to main window
my_label.pack()
main_window.mainloop()
```

**Output:**

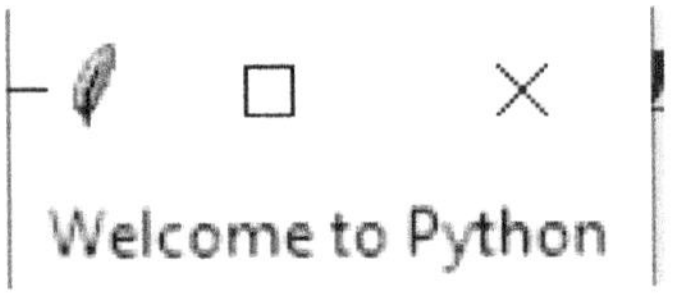


## 12.2. Working with Widgets

Widgets are GUI objects which you can use to perform different types of tasks. In the previous section, you used a label widget to display some text. In this section, you will see some other useful widgets.

Tkinter has two types of widgets: Themed widgets and normal widgets. Themed widgets are located inside the tkk module of the Tkinter library. Normal widgets are located at the top level inside the Tkinter library.

### 12.2.1. Adding a Button

The button widget allows you to add a clickable button to your window.

The following script adds a themed button named my_button to your window. To create a themed button, you need to create an object of the tkk.Button class.

The first parameter for any widget is the window to which you want to attach your widget. The other parameters are intrinsic to each widget. For instance, for the themed button, you can specify the button text via the text attribute.

You can also specify the callback function that is called when you click the button using the command attribute. Finally, you need to call the pack() method on all the widgets that you need to attach to your main window. For reference, look at the following script.

**Script 4:**

```
# importing tkinter
from tkinter import *

# importing themed tkinter
from tkinter import ttk

# defining the callback function
def my_func():
    print("a button is clicked")
```

```
# creating instance of Tk class
main_window = Tk()


# setting window dimensions
main_window.geometry("500x500+100+200")

# creating a themed button
my_button = ttk.Button(main_window,
        text = "Click here",
        command = my_func
        )

# attaching themed button to main window
my_button.pack()

main_window.mainloop()
```

**Output:**

```
a button is clicked
```

### 12.2.2. Adding a Text Field

Let's add a text field to a window. To add a text field, you can use the Entry widget. The Entry widget is available as a simple widget as well as a themed widget.

Apart from the main window attribute, you can bind the text entered in the Entry field to an object of StringVar using the textvariable attribute of the Entry class.

The following script initializes a StringVar class object named my_text. Next, an object of Entry class, i.e., text_field, is defined, which creates a text field. Look at the attributes of the Entry class. The first parameter value, as usual, is the window to which the text field will be attached. The second parameter is the my_text object, which is assigned to the textvariable attribute. If you want to retrieve the text entered in the textvariable, you can call the get() method via the my_test object.

Finally, you can call the pack() method via the text_field object. Notice here you passed True as the value for the expand attribute, which will expand the widget to the full width of the main window.

**Script 5:**

```
# importing tkinter
from tkinter import *

# importing themed tkinter
from tkinter import ttk
```

```
# creating instance of Tk class
main_window = Tk()

# setting window dimensions
main_window.geometry("500x500+100+200")

# creating variable that contains text from the text field
my_text = StringVar()

# creating a text field using Entry class
text_field = ttk.Entry(main_window, textvariable = my_text)

# addding the text field to the main window
text_field.pack(fill = 'x', expand = True)



main_window.mainloop()
```

**Output:**

Let's take a look at another example of a text field.

The following script adds two widgets to your main window. The first one is a text field, and the second one is a button. The callback function for the button is my_func(). When the button is clicked, the text of the text field is retrieved using the get() method. If the text field is empty, the user will be prompted to enter some text in the field; else, the text in the field is displayed on the console.

**Script 6:**

```
# importing tkinter
from tkinter import *

# importing themed tkinter
from tkinter import ttk

# creating instance of Tk class
main_window = Tk()

# setting window dimensions
main_window.geometry("500x500+100+200")

# creating variable that contains text from the text field
my_text = StringVar()

# creating a text field using Entry class
text_field = ttk.Entry(main_window, textvariable = my_text)

# addding the text field to the main window
text_field.pack(fill = 'x', expand = True)

def my_func():
    if my_text.get() == "":
        print("Enter something in the text box")
    else:
        print("You entered:", my_text.get())
```

```
# creating a themed button
my_button = ttk.Button(main_window,
        text ="Click here",
        command =my_func
        )

# attaching themed button to main window
my_button.pack(fill = 'x', expand = True)

main_window.mainloop()
```

**Output:**

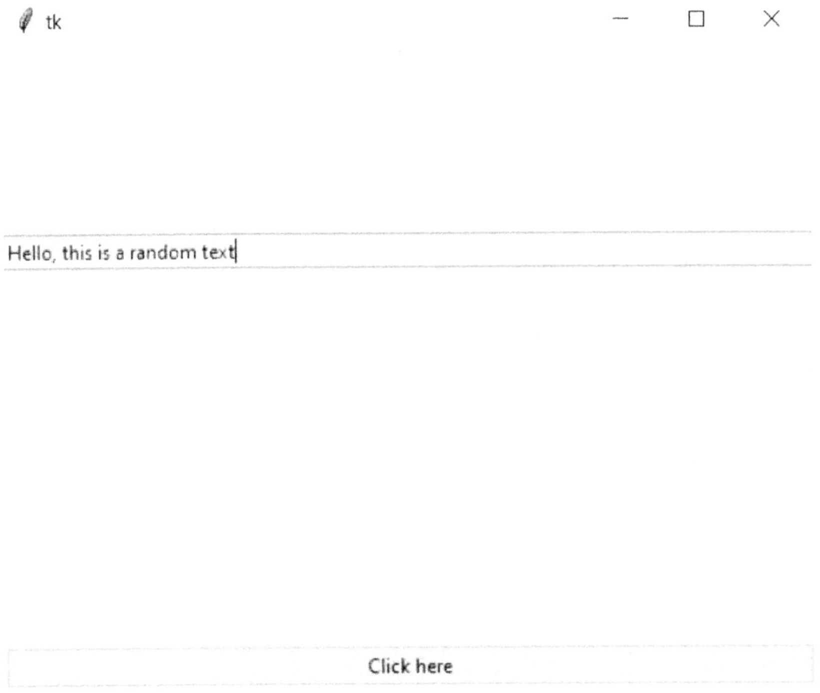


```
You entered: Hello, this is a random text
```

### 12.2.3. Adding a Message Box

A message box is used to display a message in a separate window. To display a message box, you can call the showinfo() method. The message that you want to display via the message box is passed to the message attribute.

In the following script, you add a button widget to the main window. When the button is clicked, a message is displayed on the message box that reads *You clicked a button.*

**Script 7:**

```
# importing tkinter
from tkinter import *

# importing themed tkinter
from tkinter import ttk

# importing showinfor message box
from tkinter.messagebox import showinfo

# creating instance of Tk class
main_window = Tk()

# setting window dimensions
main_window.geometry("500x500+100+200")

def my_func():
    showinfo(
        title = "Information",
        message = "You clicked a button"
    )

# creating a themed button
my_button = ttk.Button(main_window,
        text = "Click here",
        command = my_func
        )
```

```
# attaching themed button to main window
my_button.pack(fill = 'x', expand = True)

main_window.mainloop()
```

**Output:**

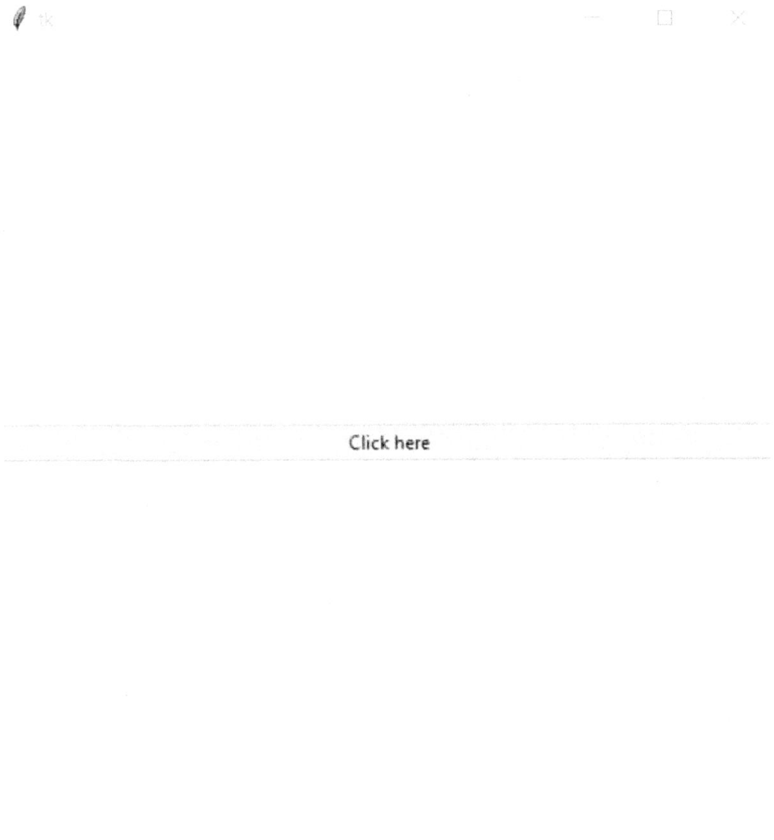


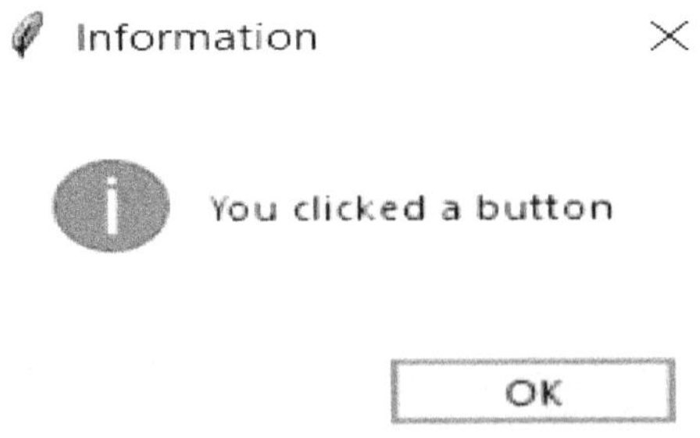

## 12.2.4. Adding Multiple Widgets

You can also add multiple widgets to a window. The process is simple. You have to create an object for each widget class. Next, you need to pass the window to which you want to attach your widgets as the first parameter. Finally, you need to call the pack() method using each widget class object.

In the following script, you add a simple label widget and a themed button widget to your main window. When the button is clicked, a message is displayed on the console.

**Script 8:**

```
# importing tkinter
from tkinter import *

# importing themed tkinter
from tkinter import ttk

# defining the callback function
def my_func():
    print("a button is clicked")

# creating instance of Tk class
main_window = Tk()


# setting window dimensions
main_window.geometry("500x500+100+200")

# creating the default label
my_label = Label(main_window,
        text = "Welcome to Python")

# attaching default label to main window
my_label.pack()
```

```
# creating a themed button
my_button = ttk.Button(main_window,
        text ="Click here",
        command =my_func
        )

# attaching themed button to main window
my_button.pack()

main_window.mainloop()
```

**Output:**

```
a button is clicked
```

Similarly, the following script adds a normal label widget, a themed label widget, and a themed button to your main window. When you click the button, a message is displayed on the console.

**Script 9:**

```
# importing tkinter
from tkinter import *

# importing themed tkinter
from tkinter import ttk

# defining the callback function
def my_func():
    print("a button is clicked")

# creating instance of Tk class
main_window = Tk()

# setting window dimensions
main_window.geometry("500x500+100+200")

# creating the default label
my_label = Label(main_window,
        text = "Welcome to Python")

# attaching default label to main window
my_label.pack()

# creating a themed label
my_label2 = ttk.Label(main_window,
        text = "Welcome to Python2")

# attaching themed label to main window
my_label2.pack()

# creating a themed button
my_button = ttk.Button(main_window,
        text = "Click here",
        command = my_func
        )
```

```
# attaching themed button to main window
my_button.pack()

main_window.mainloop()
```

**Output:**

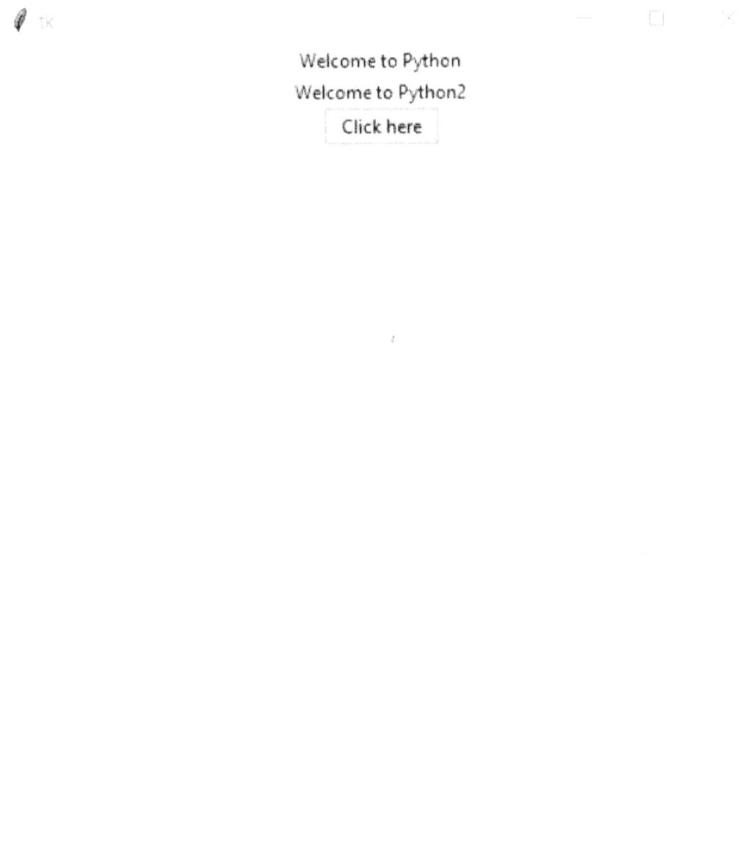


```
a button is clicked
```

Let's see another example of adding multiple widgets.

The script below adds a themed Entry and a themed Button widget to the main window. When the button is clicked, the text entered in the text field defined by the Entry widget is displayed in a message box.

**Script 10:**

```
# importing tkinter
from tkinter import *

# importing themed tkinter
from tkinter import ttk

# creating instance of Tk class
main_window = Tk()

# setting window dimensions
main_window.geometry("500x500+100+200")

# creating variable that contains text from the text field
my_text = StringVar()

# creating a text field using Entry class
text_field = ttk.Entry(main_window, textvariable = my_text)

# addding the text field to the main window
text_field.pack(fill = 'x', expand = True)

def my_func():

        text = ""
    if my_text.get()=="":
        text = "Enter something in the text box"
    else:
        text = "You entered:"+my_text.get()

# creating a message box
showinfo(title = "Information", message = text)

# creating a themed button
my_button = ttk.Button(main_window,
        text = "Click here",
        command = my_func
        )
```

```
# attaching themed button to main window
my_button.pack(fill = 'x', expand = True)

main_window.mainloop()
```

**Output:**

## 12.3. Creating a Layout

Layouts help you organize your widget in a specific way.

The following script creates a grid layout with two rows and three columns.

To create a grid layout, you only need to define the position and width of each column via the columnconfigure() method of the Tk class object (which is also your main window).

The first parameter value to the columnconfigure() is the column position. The first column position should be 0. You can also specify the value for the weight parameter, which corresponds to the span of the column.

For instance, in the following script, you create three columns with a weight of 1. If you set the weight of any column to 2, the width for that column will be twice that of the column with weight 1.

You do not have to specify values for rows. Rows will be automatically added when you attach a widget to the main window. To attach a widget to the main window, you need to call the grid() method and pass the position for the row and column indexes where you want to position your widget.

The row index is specified via the row attribute of a widget. Similarly, the column index is specified via the column attribute. The row and column indexes start from 0. For instance, row and column values of 0 will position the widget in the first row and first column.

The following script adds two labels to the main window. The first label is positioned at the first row and first column index. The second label is positioned in the first row and second column.

The following script also adds two buttons to the main window. The first button is positioned in the first row and third column. The second button is placed in the second row and first column. Notice that when you call the grid() method via the second Button widget object, i.e., my_button2, you pass a value of 3 for the columnspan attribute. The columnspan attribute defines how many spans a widget will take. A columnspan of 3 specifies the position of the cell at row and column index and increases its span to three columns.

Look at the following script for reference.

**Script 11:**

```
# importing tkinter
from tkinter import *

# importing themed tkinter
from tkinter import ttk

# creating instance of Tk class
main_window = Tk()

# setting window dimensions
main_window.geometry("500x500+100+200")

# configure the grid
main_window.columnconfigure(0, weight = 1)
main_window.columnconfigure(1, weight = 1)
main_window.columnconfigure(2, weight = 1)

# creating the default label
my_label = Label(main_window,
        text ="Welcome to Python")

# attaching label to first row and first column
my_label.grid(column=0, row=0, padx=5, pady=5)
```

```
# creating a themed label
my_label2 = ttk.Label(main_window,
        text = "Welcome to Python2")

# attaching label to first row and second column
my_label2.grid(column=1, row=0, padx=5, pady=5)

# creating a themed button
my_button = ttk.Button(main_window,
        text ="Click here"
)

# attaching a button to first row and third  column
my_button.grid(column=2, row=0, padx=5, pady=5)


# creating a themed button
my_button2 = ttk.Button(main_window,
        text = "This button spans three columns and will be
    centered horizontally",
        )

# attaching a button to first row and third  column
my_button2.grid(column=0, row=1, columnspan=3, padx=5, pady=5)

main_window.mainloop()
```

**Output:**

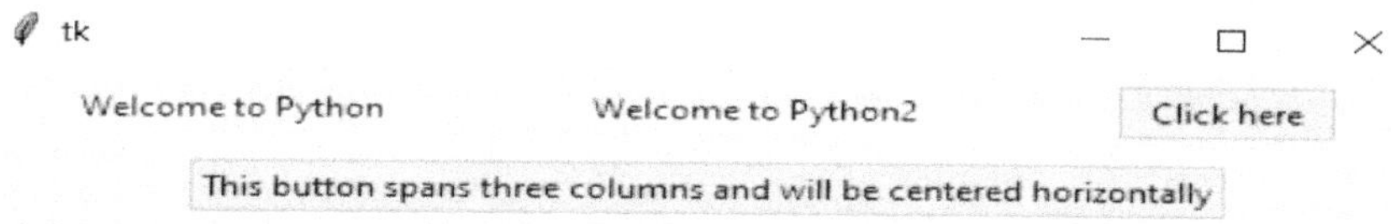

**Further Readings - Python GUI with Tkinter**

To study more about creating GUI with the Python Tkinter module, please check the official Python documentation (https://bit.ly/3aDwICG). Get used to searching and reading this documentation. It is a great resource of knowledge.

**Hands-on Time - Exercise**

Now, it is your turn. Follow the instructions in **the exercises below** to check your understanding of GUI programming with the Python Tkinter module. The answers to these questions are given at the end of the book.

# Exercise 12.1

**Question 1:**

You need to call the mainloop() method from the object of the Tk class in Tkinter because:

A. It opens the main GUI window

B. It keeps the GUI window open

C. It allows users to interact with widgets

D. None of the above

**Question 2:**

Which method is used to display a message box in the Python Tkinter module?

A. showmessage()

B. displaymessage()

C. showinfo()

D. displayinfo()

**Question 3:**

What is the distance of the Tkinter window drawn using the geometry method geometry("500x500+100+300") from the top of the screen?

A. 500

B. 100

C. 200

D. 300

## Exercise 12.2

Create a simple login form that looks like the one in the following image, using Tkinter.

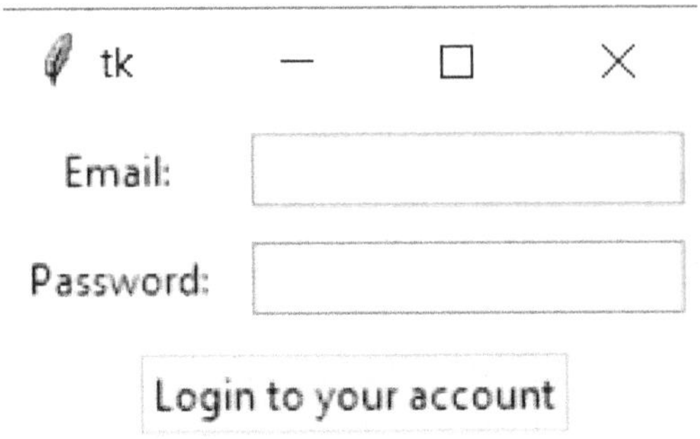


When you click the `Login to your account` button, the email should be displayed in a message box.

# 13

# Useful Python Libraries for Data Science

Data science is a field of study that uses scientific approaches and mathematical techniques such as statistics to extract meaning and insights from data. As per Dr. Thomas Miller from Northwestern University, data science is "a combination of information technology, modeling, and business management."

In this chapter, you will study three very useful libraries for data science, namely: NumPy, Pandas, and Matplotlib. The NumPy library is commonly used for performing complex mathematical operations on data. The Pandas library is used for data preprocessing, analysis, and manipulation tasks. Finally, the Matplotlib library is commonly used for data visualization and plotting.

## 13.1. NumPy Library for Numerical Computing

NumPy (Numerical Python-https://numpy.org/) is Python's library for data science and numerical computing. Many advanced data science and machine learning libraries require data to be in the form of NumPy arrays before it can be processed. NumPy comes prebuilt with Anaconda's distribution of Python. Else, you can install NumPy with the following pip command in a terminal or a command prompt:

```
$ pip install numpy
```

A NumPy array has many advantages over regular Python lists. Some of them are enlisted below:

1. NumPy arrays are much faster for insertion, deletion, update, and reading of data.
2. NumPy arrays contain advanced broadcasting functionalities compared with regular Python arrays.
3. NumPy array comes with a lot of methods that support advanced arithmetic and linear algebra options.
4. NumPy provides advanced multi-dimensional array slicing capabilities.

### 13.1.1. Creating NumPy Arrays

Depending upon the type of data you need inside your NumPy array, different methods can be used to create a NumPy array.

#### § Using Array Method

To create a NumPy array, you can pass a list to the array() method of the NumPy module, as shown below:

**Script 1:**

```
import numpy as np
nums_list = [10,12,14,16,20]
nums_array = np.array(nums_list)
type(nums_array)
```

**Output:**

```
numpy.ndarray
```

You can also create a multi-dimensional NumPy array. To do so, you need to create a list of lists where each internal list corresponds to the row in a 2-dimensional array. Here is an example of how to create a 2-dimensional array using the array() method.

**Script 2:**

```
row1 =[10,12,13]
row2 =[45,32,16]
row3 =[45,32,16]

nums_2d =np.array([row1, row2, row3])
nums_2d.shape
```

**Output:**

```
(3, 3)
```

## § Using Arange Method

With the arange () method, you can create a NumPy array that contains a range of integers. The first parameter to the Arange method is the lower bound, and the second parameter is the upper bound. The lower bound is included in the array. However, the upper bound is not included. The following script creates a NumPy array with integers 5 to 10.

**Script 3:**

```
nums_arr=np.arange(5,11)
    print(nums_arr)
```

**Output:**

```
[ 5  6  7  8  9 10]
```

You can also specify the step as a third parameter in the arange() function. A step defines the distance between the two consecutive points in the array. The following script creates a NumPy array from 5 to 11 with a step size of 2.

**Script 4:**

```
nums_arr=np.arange(5,12,2)
    print(nums_arr)
```

**Output:**

```
[ 5  7  9 11]
```

## § Using Ones Method

The ones() method can be used to create a NumPy array of all ones. Here is an example.

**Script 5:**

```
ones_array=np.ones(6)
    print(ones_array)
```

**Output:**

```
[1. 1. 1. 1. 1. 1.]
```

You can create a 2-dimensional array of all ones by passing the number of rows and columns as first and second parameters of the ones() method, as shown below:

**Script 6:**

```
ones_array=np.ones((6,4))
    print(ones_array)
```

**Output:**

```
[[1. 1. 1. 1.]
[1. 1. 1. 1.]
[1. 1. 1. 1.]
[1. 1. 1. 1.]
[1. 1. 1. 1.]
[1. 1. 1. 1.]]
```

## § Using Random Method

The random.rand() function from the NumPy module can be used to create a NumPy array with uniform distribution.

**Script 7:**

```
uniform_random=np.random.rand(4,5)
    print(uniform_random)
```

**Output:**

```
[[0.36728531 0.25376281 0.05039624 0.96432236 0.08579293]
 [0.29194804 0.93016399 0.88781312 0.50209692 0.63069239]
 [0.99952044 0.44384871 0.46041845 0.10246553 0.53461098]
 [0.75817916 0.36505441 0.01683344 0.9887365  0.21490949]]
```

The random.randn() function from the NumPy module can be used to create a NumPy array with normal distribution, as shown in the following example.

**Script 8:**

```
normal_random=np.random.randn(4,5)
    print(uniform_random)
```

**Output:**

```
[[0.36728531 0.25376281 0.05039624 0.96432236 0.08579293]
 [0.29194804 0.93016399 0.88781312 0.50209692 0.63069239]
 [0.99952044 0.44384871 0.46041845 0.10246553 0.53461098]
 [0.75817916 0.36505441 0.01683344 0.9887365  0.21490949]]
```

Finally, the random.randint() function from the NumPy module can be used to create a NumPy array with random integers between a certain range. The first parameter to the randint() function specifies the lower bound, the second parameter specifies the upper bound, while the last parameter specifies the number of random integers to be generated between the range. The following example generates five random integers between 5 and 50.

**Script 9:**

```
integer_random=np.random.randint(10,50,5)
    print(integer_random)
```

**Output:**

```
[25 49 21 35 17]
```

## 13.1.2. Reshaping NumPy Arrays

A NumPy array can be reshaped using the **reshape()** function. It is important to mention that the product of the rows and columns in the reshaped array must be equal to the product of rows and columns in the original array. For instance, in the following example, the original array contains 4 rows and 6 columns, i.e., 4 x 6 = 24. The reshaped array contains 3 rows and 8 columns, i.e., 3 x 8 = 24.

**Script 10:**

```
uniform_random=np.random.rand(4,6)
uniform_random=uniform_random.reshape(3,8)
    print(uniform_random)
```

**Output:**

```
[[0.37576967 0.5425328  0.56087883 0.35265748 0.19677258
   0.65107479  0.63287089 0.70649913]
 [0.47830882 0.3570451  0.82151482 0.09622735 0.1269332
   0.65866216  0.31875221 0.91781242]
 [0.89785438 0.47306848 0.58350797 0.4604004  0.62352155
   0.88064432  0.0859386  0.51918485]]
```

## 13.1.3. Array Indexing and Slicing

NumPy arrays can be indexed and sliced. Slicing an array means dividing an array into multiple parts.

NumPy arrays are indexed just like normal lists. Indexes in NumPy arrays start from 0, which means that the first item of a NumPy array is stored at the 0th index.

The following script creates a simple NumPy array of the first 10 positive integers.

**Script 11:**

```
s =np.arange(1,11)
    print(s)
```

**Output:**

```
[ 1  2  3  4  5  6  7  8  9 10]
```

The item at index one can be accessed as follows:

**Script 12:**

```
print(s[1])
```

**Output:**

```
2
```

To slice an array, you have to pass the lower index followed by a colon and the upper index. The items from the lower index (inclusive) to the upper index (exclusive) will be filtered.

The following script slices the array "s" from the 1st index to the 9th index. The elements from index 1 to 8 are printed in the output.

**Script 13:**

```
print(s[1:9])
```

**Output:**

```
[2 3 4 5 6 7 8 9]
```

If you specify only the upper bound, all the items from the first index to the upper bound are returned. Similarly, if you specify only the lower bound, all the items from the lower bound to the last item of the array are returned.

**Script 14:**

```
print(s[:5])
print(s[5:])
```

**Output:**

```
[1 2 3 4 5]
[ 6  7  8  9 10]
```

Array slicing can also be applied on a 2-dimensional array. To do so, you have to apply slicing on arrays and columns separately. A comma separates the rows and column slicing.

In the following script, the rows from the first and second indexes are returned, while all the columns are returned. You can see the first two complete rows in the output.

**Script 15:**

```
row1 =[10,12,13]
row2 =[45,32,16]
row3 =[45,32,16]

nums_2d =np.array([row1, row2, row3])
    print(nums_2d[:2,:])
```

**Output:**

```
[[10 12 13]
[45 32 16]]
```

Similarly, the following script returns all the rows but only the first two columns.

**Script 16:**

```
row1 =[10,12,13]
row2 =[45,32,16]
row3 =[45,32,16]

nums_2d =np.array([row1, row2, row3])
    print(nums_2d[:,:2])
```

**Output:**

```
[[10 12]
[45 32]
[45 32]]
```

Let's see another example of slicing. Here, we will slice the rows from row 1 to the end of the row and column 1 to the end of the column (remember row and column numbers start from 0). In the output, you will see the last two rows and the last two columns.

**Script 17:**

```
row1 =[10,12,13]
row2 =[45,32,16]
row3 =[45,32,16]

nums_2d =np.array([row1, row2, row3])
    print(nums_2d[1:,1:])
```

**Output:**

```
[[32 16]
[32 16]]
```

### 13.1.4. NumPy for Arithmetic Operations

NumPy arrays provide a variety of functions to perform arithmetic operations. Some of these functions are explained in this section.

#### § Finding Square Roots

The sqrt()function is used to find the square roots of all the elements in a list, as shown below:

**Script 18:**

```
nums=[10,20,30,40,50]
np_sqr=np.sqrt(nums)
    print(np_sqr)
```

**Output:**

```
[3.16227766 4.47213595 5.47722558 6.32455532 7.07106781]
```

#### § Finding Logs

The log() function is used to find the logs of all the elements in a list, as shown below:

**Script 19:**

```
nums=[10,20,30,40,50]
np_log= np.log(nums)
    print(np_log)
```

**Output:**

```
[2.30258509 2.99573227 3.40119738 3.68887945 3.91202301]
```

#### § Finding Exponents

The **exp()** function takes the exponents of all the elements in a list, as shown below:

**Script 20:**

```
nums=[10,20,30,40,50]
np_exp=np.exp(nums)
    print(np_exp)
```

**Output:**

```
[2.20264658e+04 4.85165195e+08 1.06864746e+13 2.35385267e+17
5.18470553e+21]
```

## § Finding Sine and Cosine

You can find the sines and cosines of items in a list using the sine and cosine function, respectively, as shown in the following script.

**Script 21:**

```
nums=[10,20,30,40,50]
np_sine=np.sin(nums)
    print(np_sine)

nums=[10,20,30,40,50]
np_cos=np.cos(nums)
    print(np_cos)
```

**Output:**

```
[-0.54402111  0.91294525 -0.98803162  0.74511316 -0.26237485]
[-0.83907153  0.40808206  0.15425145 -0.66693806  0.96496603]
```

### 13.1.5. NumPy for Linear Algebra Operations

Data science makes extensive use of linear algebra. The support for performing advance linear algebra functions in a fast and efficient way makes NumPy one of the most commonly used libraries for data science. In this section, you will perform some of the most linear algebraic operations with NumPy.

## § Finding Matrix Dot Product

To find a matrix dot product, you can use the dot() function. To find the dot product, the number of columns in the first matrix must match the number of rows in the second matrix.

Here is an example.

**Script 22:**

```
A =np.random.randn(4,5)

B =np.random.randn(5,4)

Z =  np.dot(A,B)

    print(Z)
```

**Output:**

```
[[ 1.43837722 -4.74991285  1.42127048 -0.41569506]
 [-1.64613809  5.79380984 -1.33542482  1.53201023]
 [-1.31518878  0.72397674 -2.01300047  0.61651047]
 [-1.36765444  3.83694475 -0.56382045  0.21757162]]
```

## § Element-Wise Matrix Multiplication

In addition to finding the dot product of two matrices, you can element-wise multiply two matrices. To do so, you can use the multiply() function. The dimensions of the two matrices must match.

**Script 23:**

```
row1 =[10,12,13]
row2 =[45,32,16]
row3 =[45,32,16]

nums_2d =np.array([row1, row2, row3])
multiply =np.multiply(nums_2d, nums_2d)
    print(multiply)
```

**Output:**

```
[[ 100  144  169]
 [2025 1024  256]
 [2025 1024  256]]
```

## § Finding Matrix Inverse

You find the inverse of a matrix via the linalg.inv() function, as shown below:

**Script 24:**

```
row1 =[1,2,3]
row2 =[4,5,6]
row3 =[7,8,9]

nums_2d =np.array([row1, row2, row3])

inverse =np.linalg.inv(nums_2d)
    print(inverse)
```

**Output:**

```
[[ 3.15251974e+15 -6.30503948e+15  3.15251974e+15]
 [-6.30503948e+15  1.26100790e+16 -6.30503948e+15]
 [ 3.15251974e+15 -6.30503948e+15  3.15251974e+15]]
```

## § Finding Matrix Determinant

Similarly, the determinant of a matrix can be found using the linalg.det() function, as shown below:

**Script 25:**

```
row1 =[1,2,3]
row2 =[4,5,6]
row3 =[7,8,9]

nums_2d =np.array([row1, row2, row3])

determinant =np.linalg.det(nums_2d)
    print(determinant)
```

**Output:**

```
-9.51619735392994e-16
```

### § Finding Matrix Trace

The trace of a matrix refers to the sum of all the elements along the diagonal of a matrix. To find the trace of a matrix, you can use the trace() function, as shown below:

**Script 26:**

```
row1 =[1,2,3]
row2 =[4,5,6]
row3 =[7,8,9]

nums_2d =np.array([row1, row2, row3])

trace =np.trace(nums_2d)
    print(trace)
```

**Output:**

```
15
```

**Further Readings – Python NumPy Module**

To study more about the Python NumPy module, please check the official documentation (https://numpy.org/). Get used to searching and reading this documentation. It is a great resource of knowledge.

## 13.2. Pandas Library for Data Analysis

In this section, you will see how to use Python's Pandas library for data analysis. In the next section, you will see how to use the Pandas library for data visualization by plotting different types of plots.

Execute the following script on your command prompt to download the Pandas library:

```
$ pip install pandas
```

The following script imports Pandas library in your application. Execute the script at the top of all Python codes that are provided in this chapter.

```
Import pandas as pd
```

### 13.2.1. Reading Data into Pandas Dataframe

You can import different types of files into a Pandas dataframe, which is a tabular structure that stores data.

The following script reads the *titanic_data.csv* file from the *Resources* folder. The first five rows of the Titanic dataset have been printed via the head() method of the Pandas dataframe containing the Titanic dataset.

**Script 27:**

```
import pandas as pd
titanic_data=pd.read_csv(r"E:\Datasets\titanic_data.csv")
titanic_data.head()
```

**Output:**

| | PassengerId | Survived | Pclass | Name | Sex | Age | SibSp | Parch | Ticket | Fare | Cabin | Embarked |
|---|---|---|---|---|---|---|---|---|---|---|---|---|
| 0 | 1 | 0 | 3 | Braund, Mr. Owen Harris | male | 22.0 | 1 | 0 | A/5 21171 | 7.2500 | NaN | S |
| 1 | 2 | 1 | 1 | Cumings, Mrs. John Bradley (Florence Briggs Th... | female | 38.0 | 1 | 0 | PC 17599 | 71.2833 | C85 | C |
| 2 | 3 | 1 | 3 | Heikkinen, Miss. Laina | female | 26.0 | 0 | 0 | STON/O2. 3101282 | 7.9250 | NaN | S |
| 3 | 4 | 1 | 1 | Futrelle, Mrs. Jacques Heath (Lily May Peel) | female | 35.0 | 1 | 0 | 113803 | 53.1000 | C123 | S |
| 4 | 5 | 0 | 3 | Allen, Mr. William Henry | male | 35.0 | 0 | 0 | 373450 | 8.0500 | NaN | S |

The read_csv() method reads data from a CSV or TSV file and stores it in a Pandas dataframe, which is a special object that stores data in the form of rows and columns.

### 13.2.2. Filtering Rows

To filter rows, you have to first identify the indexes of the rows to filter. For those indexes, you need to pass True to the opening and closing square brackets that follow the Pandas dataframe name.

The following script returns a series of True and False. True will be returned for indexes where the Pclass column has a value of 1.

**Script 28:**

```
titanic_pclass1=(titanic_data.Pclass==1)
titanic_pclass1
```

**Output:**

```
0      False
1       True
2      False
3       True
4      False
       ...
886    False
887     True
888    False
889     True
890    False
Name: Pclass, Length: 891, dtype: bool
```

Now the titanic_pclass1 series, which contains True or False, can be passed inside the opening and closing square brackets that follow the titanic_datadataframe. The result will be the

Titanic dataset, containing only those records where the Pclass column contains 1.

**Script 29:**

```
titanic_pclass1=(titanic_data.Pclass==1)
titanic_pclass1_data =titanic_data[titanic_pclass1]
titanic_pclass1_data.head()
```

**Output:**

| | PassengerId | Survived | Pclass | Name | Sex | Age | SibSp | Parch | Ticket | Fare | Cabin | Embarked |
|---|---|---|---|---|---|---|---|---|---|---|---|---|
| 1 | 2 | 1 | 1 | Cumings, Mrs. John Bradley (Florence Briggs Th... | male | 38.0 | 1 | 0 | PC 17599 | 71.2833 | C85 | C |
| 3 | 4 | 1 | 1 | Futrelle, Mrs. Jacques Heath (Lily May Peel) | male | 35.0 | 1 | 0 | 113803 | 53.1000 | C123 | S |
| 6 | 7 | 0 | 1 | McCarthy, Mr. Timothy J | male | 54.0 | 0 | 0 | 17463 | 51.8625 | E46 | S |
| 11 | 12 | 1 | 1 | Bonnell, Miss. Elizabeth | male | 58.0 | 0 | 0 | 113783 | 26.5500 | C103 | S |
| 23 | 24 | 1 | 1 | Sloper, Mr. William Thompson | male | 28.0 | 0 | 0 | 113788 | 35.5000 | A6 | S |

The comparison between the column values and filtering of rows can be done in a single line, as shown below:

**Script 30:**

```
titanic_pclass_data=titanic_data[titanic_data.Pclass==1]
titanic_pclass_data.head()
```

**Output:**

| | PassengerId | Survived | Pclass | Name | Sex | Age | SibSp | Parch | Ticket | Fare | Cabin | Embarked |
|---|---|---|---|---|---|---|---|---|---|---|---|---|
| 1 | 2 | 1 | 1 | Cumings, Mrs. John Bradley (Florence Briggs Th... | male | 38.0 | 1 | 0 | PC 17599 | 71.2833 | C85 | C |
| 3 | 4 | 1 | 1 | Futrelle, Mrs. Jacques Heath (Lily May Peel) | male | 35.0 | 1 | 0 | 113803 | 53.1000 | C123 | S |
| 6 | 7 | 0 | 1 | McCarthy, Mr. Timothy J | male | 54.0 | 0 | 0 | 17463 | 51.8625 | E46 | S |
| 11 | 12 | 1 | 1 | Bonnell, Miss. Elizabeth | male | 58.0 | 0 | 0 | 113783 | 26.5500 | C103 | S |
| 23 | 24 | 1 | 1 | Sloper, Mr. William Thompson | male | 28.0 | 0 | 0 | 113788 | 35.5000 | A6 | S |

Another commonly used operator to filter rows is the isin operator. The isin operator takes a list of values and returns only those rows where the column used for comparison contains values from the list passed to the isin operator as a parameter. For instance, the following script filters those rows where the age is 20, 21, or 22.

**Script 31:**

```
ages =[20,21,22]
age_dataset=titanic_data[titanic_data["Age"].isin(ages)]
age_dataset.head()
```

**Output:**

| | PassengerId | Survived | Pclass | Name | Sex | Age | SibSp | Parch | Ticket | Fare | Cabin | Embarked |
|---|---|---|---|---|---|---|---|---|---|---|---|---|
| 0 | 1 | 0 | 3 | Braund, Mr. Owen Harris | male | 22.0 | 1 | 0 | A/5 21171 | 7.25 | NaN | S |
| 12 | 13 | 0 | 3 | Saundercock, Mr. William Henry | male | 20.0 | 0 | 0 | A/5. 2151 | 8.05 | NaN | S |
| 37 | 38 | 0 | 3 | Cann, Mr. Ernest Charles | male | 21.0 | 0 | 0 | A./5. 2152 | 8.05 | NaN | S |
| 51 | 52 | 0 | 3 | Nosworthy, Mr. Richard Cater | male | 21.0 | 0 | 0 | A/4. 39886 | 7.80 | NaN | S |
| 56 | 57 | 1 | 2 | Rugg, Miss. Emily | male | 21.0 | 0 | 0 | C.A. 31026 | 10.50 | NaN | S |

You can filter rows in a Pandas dataframe based on multiple conditions using logical and (&) and or (|) operators. The following script returns those rows from the Pandas dataframe where passenger class is 1 and passenger age is 20, 21, and 22.

**Script 32:**

```
ages =[20,21,22]
ageclass_dataset=titanic_data[titanic_data["Age"].
    isin(ages)&(titanic_data["Pclass"]==1)]
ageclass_dataset.head()
```

**Output:**

| | PassengerId | Survived | Pclass | Name | Sex | Age | SibSp | Parch | Ticket | Fare | Cabin | Embarked |
|---|---|---|---|---|---|---|---|---|---|---|---|---|
| 102 | 103 | 0 | 1 | White, Mr. Richard Frasar | male | 21.0 | 0 | 1 | 35281 | 77.2875 | D26 | S |
| 151 | 152 | 1 | 1 | Pears, Mrs. Thomas (Edith Wearne) | male | 22.0 | 1 | 0 | 113776 | 66.6000 | C2 | S |
| 356 | 357 | 1 | 1 | Bowerman, Miss. Elsie Edith | male | 22.0 | 0 | 1 | 113505 | 55.0000 | E33 | S |
| 373 | 374 | 0 | 1 | Ringhini, Mr. Sante | male | 22.0 | 0 | 0 | PC 17760 | 135.6333 | NaN | C |
| 539 | 540 | 1 | 1 | Frolicher, Miss. Hedwig Margaritha | male | 22.0 | 0 | 2 | 13568 | 49.5000 | B39 | C |

### 13.2.3. Filtering Columns

To filter columns from a Pandas dataframe, you can use the filter()method. The list of columns that you want to filter is passed to the filter() method. The following script filters Name, Sex, and Age columns from the Titanic dataset and ignores all the other columns.

**Script 33:**

```
titanic_data_filter=titanic_data.filter(["Name","Sex","Age"])
titanic_data_filter.head()
```

The output below shows that the dataset now contains only the Name, Sex, and Age columns.

**Output:**

| | Name | Sex | Age |
|---|---|---|---|
| 0 | Braund, Mr. Owen Harris | male | 22.0 |
| 1 | Cumings, Mrs. John Bradley (Florence Briggs Th... | female | 38.0 |
| 2 | Heikkinen, Miss. Laina | female | 26.0 |
| 3 | Futrelle, Mrs. Jacques Heath (Lily May Peel) | female | 35.0 |
| 4 | Allen, Mr. William Henry | male | 35.0 |

In addition to filtering columns, you can also drop columns that you don't want in the dataset. To do so, you need to call the drop() method and pass it to the list of columns that you want to drop.

For instance, the following script drops the Name, Age, and Sex columns from the Titanic dataset and returns the remaining columns.

**Script 34:**

```
titanic_data_filter=titanic_data.drop(["Name","Sex","Age"],
    axis =1)
titanic_data_filter.head()
```

**Output:**

| | PassengerId | Survived | Pclass | SibSp | Parch | Ticket | Fare | Cabin | Embarked |
|---|---|---|---|---|---|---|---|---|---|
| 0 | 1 | 0 | 3 | 1 | 0 | A/5 21171 | 7.2500 | NaN | S |
| 1 | 2 | 1 | 1 | 1 | 0 | PC 17599 | 71.2833 | C85 | C |
| 2 | 3 | 1 | 3 | 0 | 0 | STON/O2. 3101282 | 7.9250 | NaN | S |
| 3 | 4 | 1 | 1 | 1 | 0 | 113803 | 53.1000 | C123 | S |
| 4 | 5 | 0 | 3 | 0 | 0 | 373450 | 8.0500 | NaN | S |

**Further Readings – Pandas Filter**

To study more about the Pandas Filter method, please check Pandas' official documentation for the filter method (https://bit.ly/2C8SWhB). Try to execute the filter method with a different set of attributes as mentioned in the official documentation.

### 13.2.4. Sorting Dataframes

To sort a Pandas dataframe, you can use the sort_values() function of the Pandas dataframe. The list of columns used for sorting needs to be passed to the **by** attribute of the sort_values() method. The following script sorts the Titanic dataset by the ascending order of the passenger's age.

**Script 35:**

```
age_sorted_data=titanic_data.sort_values(by=['Age'])
age_sorted_data.head()
```

**Output:**

| | PassengerId | Survived | Pclass | Name | Sex | Age | SibSp | Parch | Ticket | Fare | Cabin | Embarked |
|---|---|---|---|---|---|---|---|---|---|---|---|---|
| 803 | 804 | 1 | 3 | Thomas. Master. Assad Alexander | male | 0.42 | 0 | 1 | 2625 | 8.5167 | NaN | C |
| 755 | 756 | 1 | 2 | Hamalainen. Master. Viljo | male | 0.67 | 1 | 1 | 250649 | 14.5000 | NaN | S |
| 644 | 645 | 1 | 3 | Baclini, Miss. Eugenie | male | 0.75 | 2 | 1 | 2666 | 19.2583 | NaN | C |
| 469 | 470 | 1 | 3 | Baclini. Miss. Helene Barbara | male | 0.75 | 2 | 1 | 2666 | 19.2583 | NaN | C |
| 78 | 79 | 1 | 2 | Caldwell. Master. Alden Gates | male | 0.83 | 0 | 2 | 248738 | 29.0000 | NaN | S |

To sort by the descending order, you need to pass False as the value for the ascending attribute of the sort_values() function. The following script sorts the dataset by descending order of age.

**Script 36:**

```
age_sorted_data=titanic_data.sort_values(by=['Age'], ascending
    =False)
age_sorted_data.head()
```

**Output:**

| | PassengerId | Survived | Pclass | Name | Sex | Age | SibSp | Parch | Ticket | Fare | Cabin | Embarked |
|---|---|---|---|---|---|---|---|---|---|---|---|---|
| 630 | 631 | 1 | 1 | Barkworth, Mr. Algernon Henry Wilson | male | 80.0 | 0 | 0 | 27042 | 30.0000 | A23 | S |
| 851 | 852 | 0 | 3 | Svensson, Mr. Johan | male | 74.0 | 0 | 0 | 347060 | 7.7750 | NaN | S |
| 493 | 494 | 0 | 1 | Artagaveytia, Mr. Ramon | male | 71.0 | 0 | 0 | PC 17609 | 49.5042 | NaN | C |
| 96 | 97 | 0 | 1 | Goldschmidt, Mr. George B | male | 71.0 | 0 | 0 | PC 17754 | 34.6542 | A5 | C |
| 116 | 117 | 0 | 3 | Connors, Mr. Patrick | male | 70.5 | 0 | 0 | 370369 | 7.7500 | NaN | Q |

You can also pass multiple columns to the *by* attribute of the sort_values()function. In such a case, the dataset will be sorted by the first column, and in the case of equal values for two or more records, the dataset will be sorted by the second column and so on.

The following script first sorts the data by Age and then by Fare, both by descending orders.

**Script 37:**

```
age_sorted_data=titanic_data.sort_values(by=['Age','Fare'],
    ascending =False)
age_sorted_data.head()
```

**Output:**

| | PassengerId | Survived | Pclass | Name | Sex | Age | SibSp | Parch | Ticket | Fare | Cabin | Embarked |
|---|---|---|---|---|---|---|---|---|---|---|---|---|
| 630 | 631 | 1 | 1 | Barkworth, Mr. Algernon Henry Wilson | male | 80.0 | 0 | 0 | 27042 | 30.0000 | A23 | S |
| 851 | 852 | 0 | 3 | Svensson, Mr. Johan | male | 74.0 | 0 | 0 | 347060 | 7.7750 | NaN | S |
| 493 | 494 | 0 | 1 | Artagaveytia, Mr. Ramon | male | 71.0 | 0 | 0 | PC 17609 | 49.5042 | NaN | C |
| 96 | 97 | 0 | 1 | Goldschmidt, Mr. George B | male | 71.0 | 0 | 0 | PC 17754 | 34.6542 | A5 | C |
| 116 | 117 | 0 | 3 | Connors, Mr. Patrick | male | 70.5 | 0 | 0 | 370369 | 7.7500 | NaN | Q |

**Further Readings – Python Pandas Module**

To study more about the Python Pandas module, please check the official documentation (https://pandas.pydata.org/). Get used to searching and reading this documentation. It is a great resource of knowledge.

## 13.3. Matplotlib for Data Visualization

In this section, we will start a formal discussion about Aatplotlib, which is one of the most commonly and frequently used Python libraries for data visualization. Matplotlib is so popular that various advanced data visualization libraries such as Seaborn use Matplotlib as the underlying data visualization library.

Finally, before you can plot any graphs with the Matplotlib library, you will need to import the pyplot module from the Matplotlib library. And since all the scripts will be executed inside Jupyter Notebook, the statement %matplotlib inline has been used to generate plots inside Jupyter Notebook. Execute the following script:

**Script 38:**

```
import matplotlib.pyplot as plt
%matplotlib inline
```

### 13.3.1. Line Plots

The first plot that we are going to plot in this chapter is a line plot. A line plot is the simplest of all the Matplotlib plots.

A line plot is used to plot the relationship between two numerical sets of values. Usually, a line plot is used to plot an increasing or decreasing trend between two dependent variables. For instance, if you want to see how the weather changed for 24 hours, you can use a line plot where the x-axis contains hourly information and the y-axis contains the weather in degrees.

Let us plot a line plot that displays the square root of 20 equidistant numbers between 0 and 20. Look at the following script:

**Script 39:**

```
import matplotlib.pyplot as plt
import numpy as np
import math

x_vals = np.linspace(0, 20, 20)
y_vals = [math.sqrt(i) for i in x_vals]
plt.plot(x_vals, y_vals)
```

In the above script, you generate 20 equidistant numbers using np.linspace**()** function. The numbers are stored in the x_ vals variable. Next, we iterate through each value in the x_vals list and take the square root of each value. The resultant list is stored in the y_vals variable.

To plot a line plot via the pyplot module, you only need to call the plot() method of the pyplot module and then pass it the values for the x and y axes. It is important to mention that plt is an alias for pyplot in script 1. You can name it anything you want. Here is the output for script 39.

**Output:**

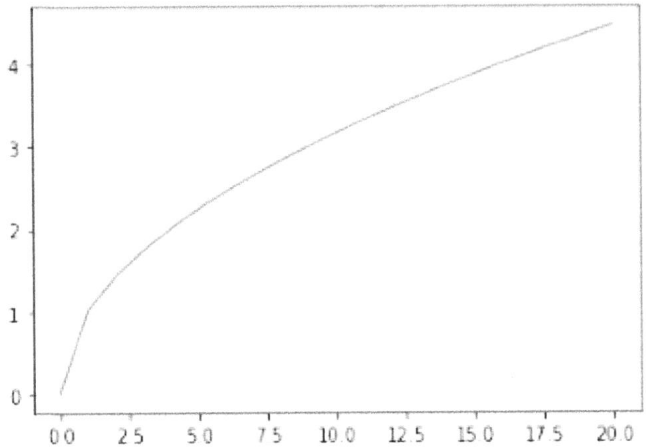


This is one of the ways to plot a graph via Matplotlib. There is also another way to do so. You have to first call the figure() method via the plt module, which draws an empty figure. Next, you can call the axes() method, which returns an axes object. You can then call the plot() method from the axes object to create a plot, as shown in the following script.

**Script 40:**

```
import matplotlib.pyplot as plt
import numpy as np
import math

x_vals = np.linspace(0, 20, 20)
y_vals = [math.sqrt(i) for i in x_vals]

fig = plt.figure()
ax = plt.axes()
ax.plot(x_vals, y_vals)
```

Here is the output of the above script. This method can be used to plot multiple plots, which we will see in the next chapter. In this chapter, we will stick to the first approach, where we call the plot() method directly from the pyplot module.

**Output:**

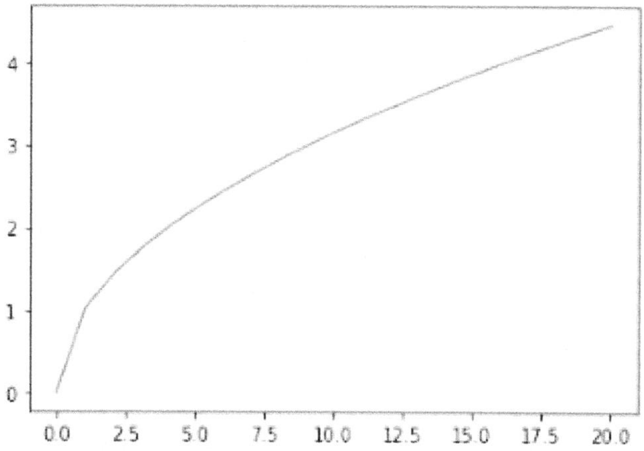


You can also increase the default plot size of a Matplotlib plot. To do so, you can use the rcParams list of the pyplot module and then set two values for the figure.figsize attribute.

The following script sets the plot size to 8 inches wide and 6 inches tall.

**Script 41:**

```
import matplotlib.pyplot as plt
import numpy as np
import math

plt.rcParams["figure.figsize"] = [8, 6]

x_vals = np.linspace(0, 20, 20)
y_vals = [math.sqrt(i) for i in x_vals]
plt.plot(x_vals, y_vals)
```

In the output, you can see that the default plot size has been increased.

**Output:**

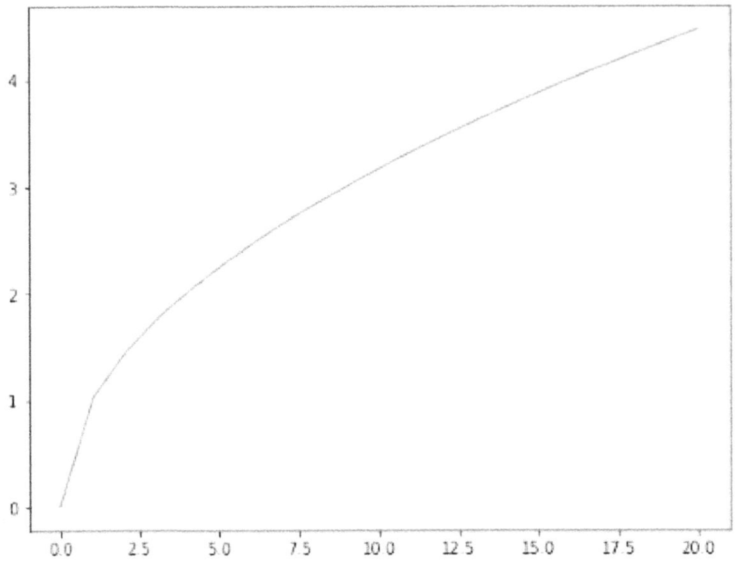


### 13.3.2. Titles Labels and Legends

You can improve the aesthetics and readability of your graphs by adding titles, labels, and legends to your graph. Let's first see how to add titles and labels to a plot.

To add labels on the x and y axes, you need to pass string values respectively to the xlabel and ylabel methods of the pyplot module. Similarly, to set a title, you need pass a string value to the title method, as shown in the following script.

**Script 42:**

```
import matplotlib.pyplot as plt
import numpy as np
import math
```

```
x_vals = np.linspace(0, 20, 20)
y_vals = [math.sqrt(i) for i in x_vals]
plt.xlabel('X Values')
plt.ylabel('Y Values')
plt.title('Square Roots')
plt.plot(x_vals, y_vals)
```

Here, in the output, you can see the labels and titles that you specified in the above script.

**Output:**

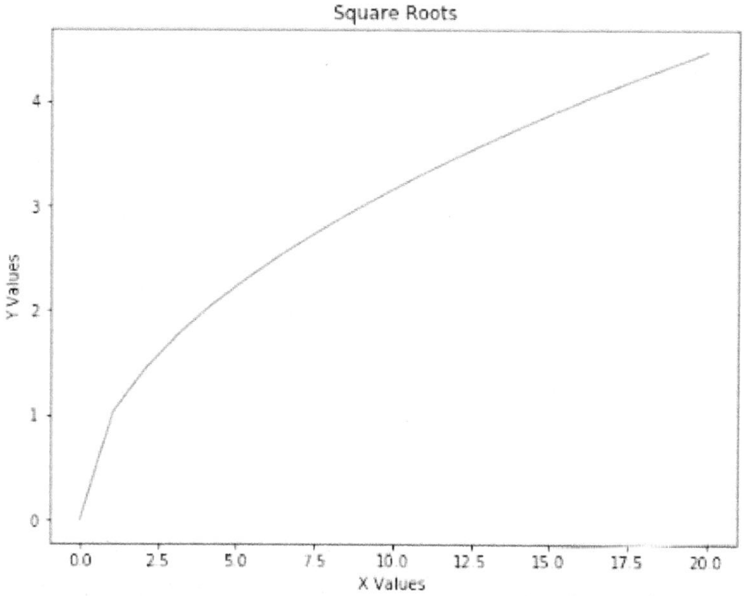


In addition to changing titles and labels, you can also specify the color for the line plot. To do so, you simply have to pass the shorthand notation for the color name to the plot() function, for example, *r* for red, *b* for blue, and so on. Here is an example:

**Script 43:**

```
import matplotlib.pyplot as plt
import numpy as np
import math
```

```
x_vals = np.linspace(0, 20, 20)
y_vals = [math.sqrt(i) for i in x_vals]
plt.xlabel('X Values')
plt.ylabel('Y Values')
plt.title('Square Roots')
plt.plot(x_vals, y_vals, 'r')
```

**Output:**

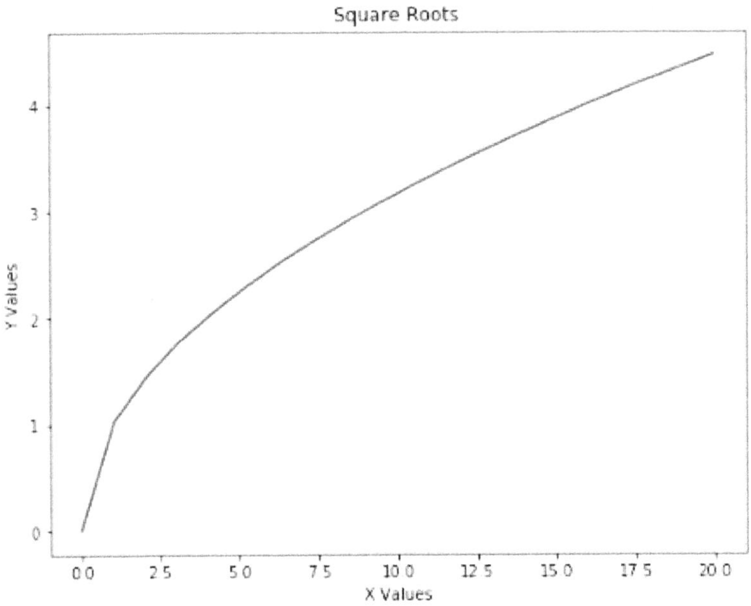


To add a legend, you need to make two changes. First, you have to pass a string value for the label attribute of the plot() function. Next, you have to pass a value for the loc attribute of the legend method of the pyplot module. In the loc attribute, you have to pass the location of your legend.

The following script plots a legend at the upper center corner of the plot.

**Script 44:**

```
import matplotlib.pyplot as plt
import numpy as np
import math

x_vals = np.linspace(0, 20, 20)
y_vals = [math.sqrt(i) for i in x_vals]
plt.xlabel('X Values')
plt.ylabel('Y Values')
plt.title('Square Roots')
plt.plot(x_vals, y_vals, 'r', label = 'Square Root')
plt.legend(loc = 'upper center')
```

**Output:**

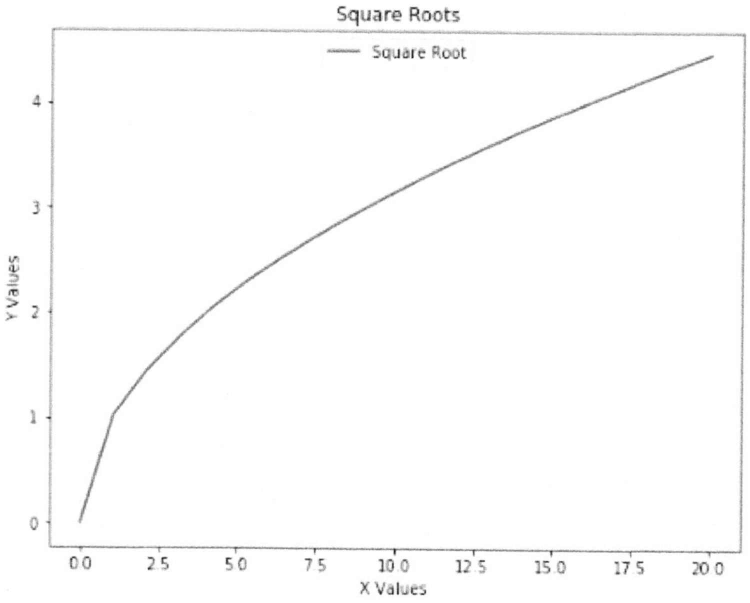


You can also plot multiple line plots inside one graph. All you have to do is call the plot() method twice with different values for the x and y axes. The following script plots a line plot for square root in red and for a cube function in blue.

### Script 45:

```
import matplotlib.pyplot as plt
import numpy as np
import math


x_vals = np.linspace(0, 20, 20)
y_vals = [math.sqrt(i) for i in x_vals]
y2_vals = x_vals ** 3
plt.xlabel('X Values')
plt.ylabel('Y Values')
plt.title('Square Roots')
plt.plot(x_vals, y_vals, 'r', label = 'Square Root')
plt.plot(x_vals, y2_vals, 'b', label = 'Cube')
plt.legend(loc = 'upper center')
```

### Output:

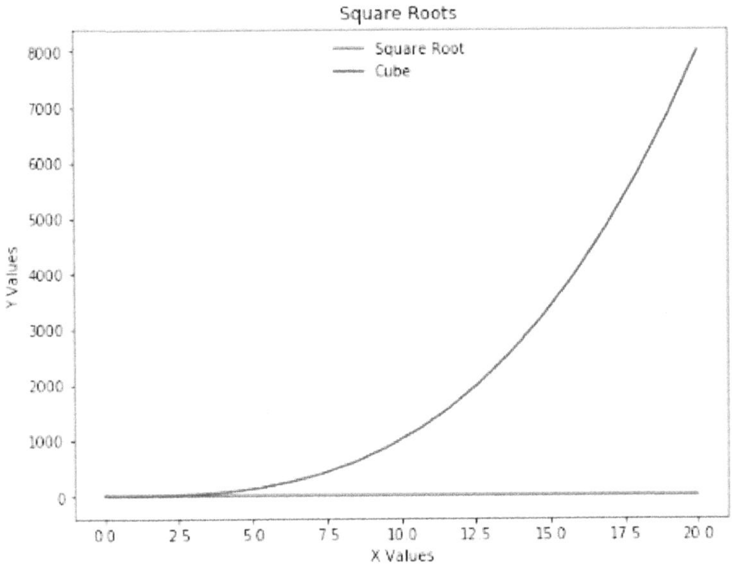

**Further Readings - Matplotlib Line Plot**

To study more about Matplotlib line plots, please check Matplotlib's official documentation for line plots (https://bit.ly/33BqsIR). Get used to searching and reading this documentation. It is a great resource of knowledge.

### 13.3.3. Scatter Plots

Scatter plot is used to plot the relationship between two numeric columns in the form of scattered points. Normally, a scattered plot is used when for each value in the x-axis, there exist multiple values in the y-axis. To plot a scatter plot, the scatter()function of the pyplot module is used. You have to pass the values for the x-axis and y-axis. In addition, you have to pass a shorthand notation of color value to the **c** parameter.

The following script shows how to plot a scatter plot between sepal length and petal length of iris plants.

**Script 46:**

```
import matplotlib.pyplot as plt
import numpy as np
import math

import pandas as pd
data = pd.read_csv("E:\Datasets\iris_data.tsv", sep = '\t')
data.head()

plt.xlabel('Sepal Length')
plt.ylabel('Petal Length')
plt.title('Sepal vs Petal Length')
plt.scatter(data["SepalLength"], data["PetalLength"], c = "b")
```

The output shows a scattered plot with blue points. The plot clearly shows that with an increase in sepal length, the petal length of an iris flower also increases.

**Output:**

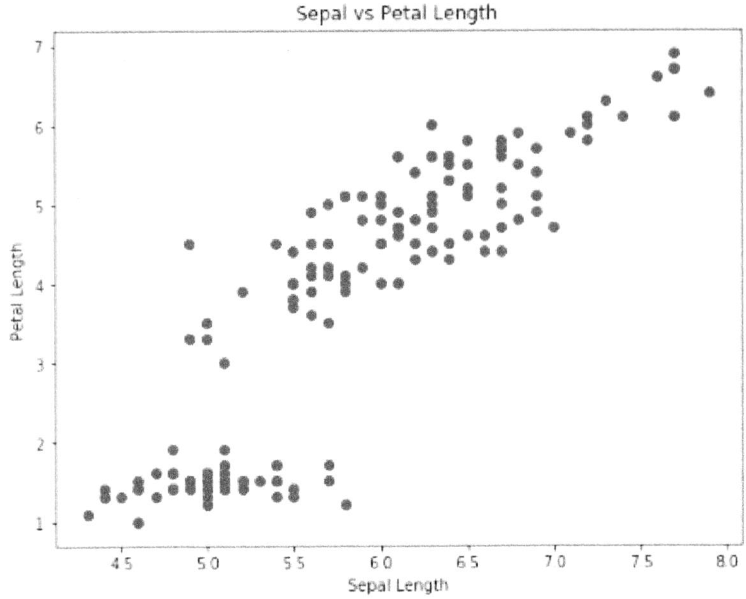


**Further Readings – Matplotlib Scatter Plot**

To study more about Matplotlib scatter plot, please check Matplotlib's official documentation for scatter plots (https://bit.ly/3a8Dtef). Get used to searching and reading this documentation. It is a great resource of knowledge.

### 13.3.4. Bar Plots

Bar plot is used to plot the relationship between unique values in a categorical column grouped by an aggregate function such as sum, mean, median, etc. Before we plot a bar plot, let's first import the dataset that we are going to use in this chapter. Execute the following script to read the **titanic_data.csv** file. You find the CSV file in the "Resources/Datasets" folder. The following script also displays the first 5 rows of the dataset.

**Script 47:**

```
import pandas as pd
data = pd.read_csv(r"E:\Data Visualization with Python\
   Datasets\titanic_data.csv")
data.head()
```

**Output:**

| | PassengerId | Survived | Pclass | Name | Sex | Age | SibSp | Parch | Ticket | Fare | Cabin | Embarked |
|---|---|---|---|---|---|---|---|---|---|---|---|---|
| 0 | 1 | 0 | 3 | Braund, Mr. Owen Harris | male | 22.0 | 1 | 0 | A/5 21171 | 7.2500 | NaN | S |
| 1 | 2 | 1 | 1 | Cumings, Mrs. John Bradley (Florence Briggs Th... | female | 38.0 | 1 | 0 | PC 17599 | 71.2833 | C85 | C |
| 2 | 3 | 1 | 3 | Heikkinen, Miss. Laina | female | 26.0 | 0 | 0 | STON/O2. 3101282 | 7.9250 | NaN | S |
| 3 | 4 | 1 | 1 | Futrelle, Mrs. Jacques Heath (Lily May Peel) | female | 35.0 | 1 | 0 | 113803 | 53.1000 | C123 | S |
| 4 | 5 | 0 | 3 | Allen, Mr. William Henry | male | 35.0 | 0 | 0 | 373450 | 8.0500 | NaN | S |

To plot a bar plot, you need to call the bar() method. The categorical values are passed as the x-axis, and corresponding aggregated numerical values are passed on the y-axis. The following script plots a bar plot between genders and ages of the Titanic ship.

**Script 48:**

```
import matplotlib.pyplot as plt
import numpy as np
import math

plt.xlabel('Gender')
plt.ylabel('Ages')
plt.title('Gender vs Age')
plt.bar(data["Sex"], data["Age"])
```

**Output:**

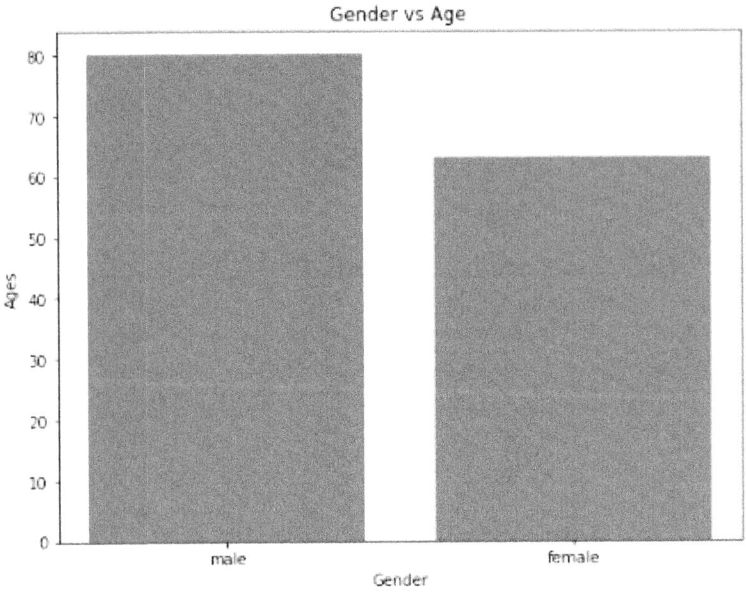


**Further Readings – Matplotlib Bar Plot**

To study more about Matplotlib bar plots, please check Matplotlib's official documentation for bar plots. (https://bit.ly/2PNKR5r). Get used to searching and reading this documentation. It is a great resource of knowledge.

## 13.3.5. Pie Charts

Pie chart, as the name suggests, displays the percentage distribution of values in a categorical column in terms of an aggregated function.

For instance, the following script shows the percentage distribution of jobs concerning job categories, i.e., IT, Marketing, Data Science, and Finance.

To plot a pie chart, the pie() method of the pyplot module. The first parameter is the list of numeric values that you want to be converted and displayed into percentages. Next, you have to pass a list of categories to the labels parameter. The explode parameter defines the magnitude of the split for each category in the pie chart. The autopctparameter defines the format in which percentage will be displayed on the pie chart. Here is an example:

**Script 49:**

```
labels ='IT','Marketing','Data Science','Finance'
values =[500,156,300,510]
explode =(0.05,0.05,0.05,0.05)

plt.pie(values, explode=explode, labels=labels,
    autopct='%1.1f%%', shadow=True)
plt.show()
```

**Output:**

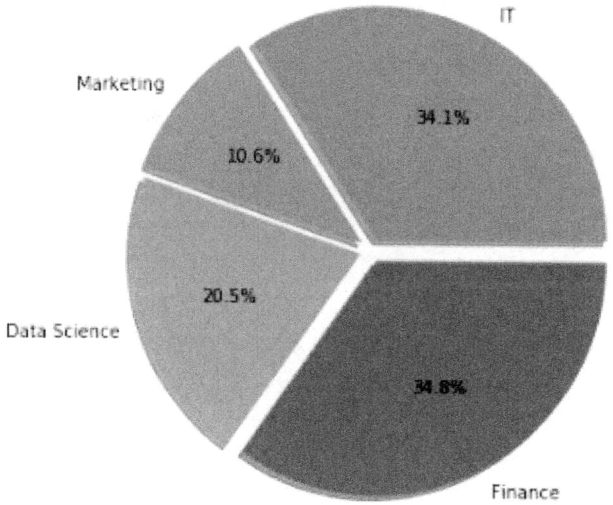

**Further Readings - Matplotlib Pie Charts**

To study more about Matplotlib Pie Charts, please check Matplotlib's official documentation for Pie Charts. (https://bit.ly/31qoXdy). Get used to searching and reading this documentation. It is a great resource of knowledge.

**Hands-on Time - Exercise**

Now, it is your turn. Follow the instructions in **the exercises below** to check your understanding of Python's NumPy, Pandas, and Matplotlib libraries for data science. The answers to these questions are given at the end of the book.

# Exercise 13.1

**Question 1:**

Which NumPy function is used for the element-wise multiplication of two matrices?

A. np.dot(matrix1, matrix2)

B. np.multiply(matrix1, matrix2)

C. np.elementwise(matrix1, matrix2)

D. None of the above

**Question 2:**

Which function is used to sort Pandas dataframe by a column value?

A. sort_dataframe()

B. sort_rows()

C. sort_values()

D. sort_records()

**Question 3:**

How to show percentage values on a Matplotlib pie chart?

A. autopct = '%1.1f%%'

B. percentage = '%1.1f%%'

C. perc = '%1.1f%%'

D. None of the Above

# Exercise 13.2

Create a random NumPy array of 5 rows and 4 columns. Using array indexing and slicing, display the items from row 3 to end and column 2 to end.

**Solution:**

```
uniform_random=np.random.rand(4,5)
print(uniform_random)
print("Result")
print(uniform_random[2:,3:])
```

## Project 1

# A Simple GUI Based Calculator in Python

You have learned all the basics of the Python programming language till now. Now is the time to put into practice what you have learned so far in this book. You will be developing three simple Python projects: A GUI-based calculator, an alarm clock, and the hangman word-guessing game.

In this first project, you will develop a simple calculator, which looks like the one in the image below. So let's begin without further ado.

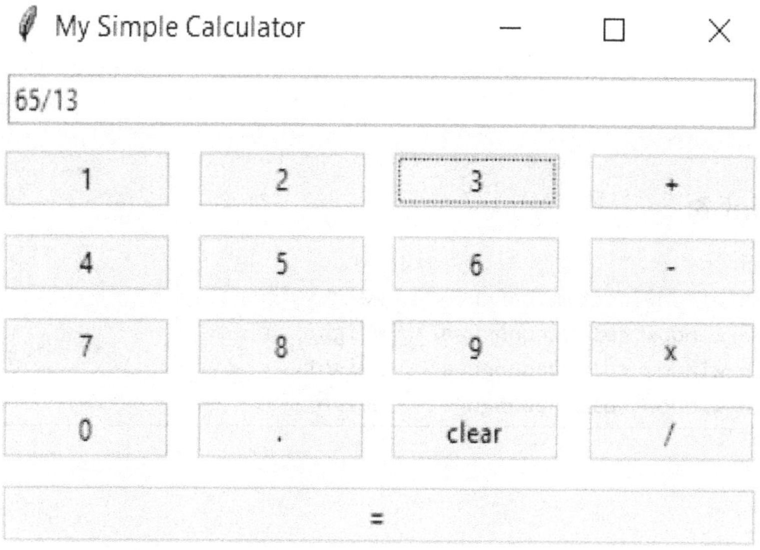

## Importing the Required Libraries

In the first step, you need to import the libraries required to develop the calculator shown in the image above. You will be using Tkinter and Tkk modules.

**Script 1:**

```
# importing tkinter
from tkinter import *

# importing tkk
from tkinter import ttk
```

## Creating Main Window

To create a GUI using Tkinter, you need to create the main window that will contain all your widgets. The following script creates the main window.

**Script 2:**

```
# creating instance of Tk class
main_window = Tk()
main_window.title("My Simple Calculator")
```

Our calculator will have four columns. The following script defines that.

**Script 3:**

```
# adding four columns to main window
main_window.columnconfigure(0, weight=1)
main_window.columnconfigure(1, weight=1)
main_window.columnconfigure(2, weight=1)
main_window.columnconfigure(3, weight=1)
```

## Adding Widgets and Logic

The first widget that you need to add is the Entry widget. This Entry widget will add a text box, which will hold your expression. The Entry widget in the first row will occupy all four columns.

Execute the following script to add a simple text field in the first row of your grid in the main window.

**Script 4:**

```
text =StringVar()
# creating a text field using Entry class
text_field=ttk.Entry(main_window,textvariable= text, width=55)

# attaching label to first row and second column
text_field.grid(row=0, column=0,columnspan=4,padx=5,pady=5)
```

The following script defines a method that will be used as a callback when the user clicks on any of the buttons except the equals button or the clear button.

The following method adds the value of the button pressed to the already existing expression.

**Script 5:**

```
expression_string = ""

def press_button(num):
    # access the global expression_string
    global expression_string

    # add new text to the existing expression_string
    expression_string = expression_string + str(num)

    # update the text field with expression_string
    text.set(expression_string)
```

The following script defines the press_equal_button() method. This method is called when the equal button is clicked. The method uses the built-in eval() method to evaluate an expression in the form of a text. For example, if the expression in the text field is "5+6", the eval() method will convert this string into a mathematical expression and will return its result.

The result of the eval() method is then displayed in the text field in the first row of the calculator. In case the expression cannot be evaluated, an error message is printed in the text field.

**Script 6:**

```
def press_equal_button():

    try:
        # access the global expression_string
        global expression_string

        # evaluate the text in expression_string
        result = str(eval(expression_string))

        # display the result in the text field
        text.set(result)

        # update expression_string to an empty string
        expression_string = ""

    except:
        # show error in case of exception
        text.set(" error ")

        # update expression_string to an empty string
        expression_string = ""
```

Finally, the clear method clears the expression string containing your calculation along with the text field that contains the expression.

**Script 7:**

```
def clear():
    # update expression_string to an empty string
    expression_string = ""

    # update text field to an empty string
    text.set("")
```

The following script adds four buttons in the second row of the grid. The buttons added are "1, 2, 3, and +". When one of these buttons is clicked, the corresponding values are passed to the callback method press_button()via the lambda expression.

**Script 8:**

```
# creating a themed button for digit 1 and attaching it to the
    main window
my_button1 = ttk.Button(main_window, text = "1", command =
    lambda:press_button(1))

my_button1.grid(row=1, column=0, padx=5, pady=5)

# creating a themed button for digit 2 and attaching it to the
    main window
my_button2 = ttk.Button(main_window, text = "2", command =
    lambda:press_button(2))

my_button2.grid(row=1, column=1, padx=5, pady=5)

# creating a themed button for digit 3 and attaching it to the
    main window
my_button3 = ttk.Button(main_window, text = "3", command =
    lambda:press_button(3))

my_button3.grid(row=1, column=2, padx=5, pady=5)
```

```
# creating a themed button for sign + and attaching it to the
    main window
my_button_plus = ttk.Button(main_window, text = "+", command =
    lambda:press_button("+"))

my_button_plus.grid(row=1, column=3, padx=5, pady=5)
```

Similarly, the following script adds four buttons in a third of the grid. The buttons added are "4, 5, 6, and –".

**Script 9:**

```
# creating a themed button for digit 4 and attaching it to the
    main window
my_button4 = ttk.Button(main_window, text = "4", command =
    lambda:press_button(4))

my_button4.grid(row=2, column=0, padx=5, pady=5)

# creating a themed button for digit 5 and attaching it to the
    main window
my_button5 = ttk.Button(main_window, text = "5", command =
    lambda:press_button(5))

my_button5.grid(row=2, column=1, padx=5, pady=5)

# creating a themed button for digit 6 and attaching it to the
    main window
my_button6 = ttk.Button(main_window, text = "6", command =
    lambda:press_button(6))

my_button6.grid(row=2, column=2, padx=5, pady=5)

# creating a themed button for sign - and attaching it to the
    main window
my_button_minus = ttk.Button(main_window, text = "-", command
    = lambda:press_button("-"))

my_button_minus.grid(row=2, column=3, padx=5, pady=5)
```

The following script adds four more buttons in the fourth row of the grid. The buttons added are “7, 8, 9, and x”.

**Script 10:**

```
# creating a themed button for digit 7 and attaching it to the
    main window
my_button7 = ttk.Button(main_window, text = "7", command =
    lambda:press_button(7))

my_button7.grid(row=3, column=0, padx=5, pady=5)

# creating a themed button for digit 8 and attaching it to the
    main window
my_button8 = ttk.Button(main_window, text = "8", command =
    lambda:press_button(8))

my_button8.grid(row=3, column=1, padx=5, pady=5)

# creating a themed button for digit 9 and attaching it to the
    main window
my_button9 = ttk.Button(main_window, text = "9", command =
    lambda:press_button(9))

my_button9.grid(row=3, column=2, padx=5, pady=5)

# creating a themed button for sign x and attaching it to the
    main window
my_button_mul = ttk.Button(main_window, text = "x", command =
    lambda:press_button("*"))

my_button_mul.grid(row=3, column=3, padx=5, pady=5)
```

Again, we add four more buttons: 0, ., clear, and / in the 5th row. The callback method for the clear button is clear().

**Script 11:**

```
# creating a themed button for digit 0 and attaching it to the
    main window
my_button0 = ttk.Button(main_window, text = "0", command =
    lambda:press_button(0))

my_button0.grid(row=4, column=0, padx=5, pady=5)

# creating a themed button for a dot and attaching it to the
    main window
my_button_dot = ttk.Button(main_window, text = ".", command =
    lambda:press_button("."))

my_button_dot.grid(row=4, column=1, padx=5, pady=5)

# creating a themed button for clear and attaching it to the
    main window
my_button_clr=ttk.Button(main_window, text = "clear", command
    = clear)

my_button_clr.grid(row=4, column=2, padx=5, pady=5)

# creating a themed button for sign / and attaching it to the
    main window
my_button_div = ttk.Button(main_window, text = "/", command =
    lambda:press_button("/"))

my_button_div.grid(row=4, column=3, padx=5, pady=5)
```

Finally, in the last row, we add the button displaying the equals sign "=". The callback method for this button is press_equal_button(), which evaluates the expression in the text field.

**Script 12:**

```
# creating a themed button for sign = and attaching it to the
    main window
my_button_eqls = ttk.Button(main_window, text = "=",  width =
    55, command = press_equal_button)
my_button_eqls.grid(row=5, column=0, columnspan=4, padx=5,
    pady=5)
```

To keep the GUI window visible during the interaction, execute the following script.

**Script 13:**

```
# displaying the main window
main_window.mainloop()
```

When you execute all of the above scripts in this project, you will see the following GUI.

To create an expression, you need click buttons. For instance, to divide 65 by 13, as shown in the following image, click button 6, followed by 5, /, 1, and 3. You will see the expression appearing in your text field. Next, click the equals "=" button, and you will see 5.0 in the text field, which is the result when you divide 65 by 13.

You can play around with the calculator and try other calculations to see if the calculator works correctly.

**Final Output**

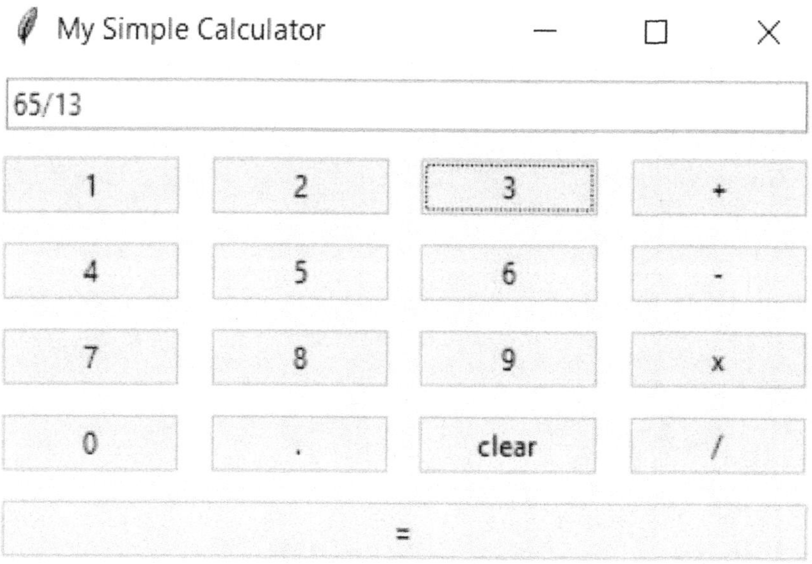

## Project 2

# Alarm Clock with Python

In this project, you will create a very simple alarm clock with Python. You will again use the Tkinter library along with other built-in Python functionalities to develop the alarm clock. Here is how your alarm clock will look.

The alarm clock will play an audio of a siren at the time you passed to the hour, minutes, and seconds fields. The time should be passed in the 24-hour time format.

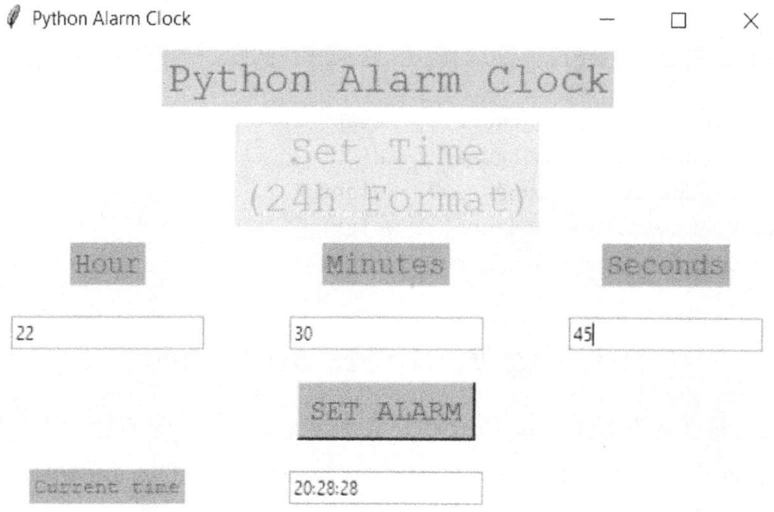


## Importing the Required Libraries

The following script imports required libraries for this project.

**Script 1:**

```
from tkinter import *
from tkinter import ttk
import datetime
import time
import winsound
from tkinter.messagebox import showinfo
from threading import*
```

## Creating Main Window

The script below creates the main window that will hold all your widgets.

**Script 2:**

```
main_window= Tk()
main_window.title("Python Alarm Clock")
```

The main window will contain five columns of equal widths.

**Script 3:**

```
# adding four columns to main window
main_window.columnconfigure(0, weight=1)
main_window.columnconfigure(1, weight=1)
main_window.columnconfigure(2, weight=1)
main_window.columnconfigure(3, weight=1)
main_window.columnconfigure(3, weight=1)
```

## Adding Widgets and Logic

First, you will add two labels at the top of the GUI. The first label will contain the text *Python Alarm Click*. The second label will display the text *Set Time*.

In the script below, the bg, fg, and font attributes of the Label class are used to set the background color, the foreground color, and the font type and size, respectively.

**Script 4:**

```
# creating a label for title and attaching it the main window
my_label= Label(main_window, text ="Python Alarm
    Clock",bg="#b3b3b3",fg="#ff3300", font=("Courier",20))
my_label.grid(row=0, column=1,columnspan=3,padx=5,pady=5)

# creating a label for a message and attaching it the main
    window
my_labe2 = Label(main_window, text ="Set Time\n(24h
    Format)",bg="#cccccc",fg="#3399ff", font=("Courier",20))
my_labe2.grid(row=1, column=2,padx=5,pady=5)
```

The following script adds three labels. The labels display *Hour, Minutes*, *Seconds*.

**Script 5:**

```
# creating a label for hours and attaching it the main window
lbl_hours= Label(main_window, text
    ="Hour",bg="#6699ff",fg="#595959", font=("Courier",14))
lbl_hours.grid(row=2, column=1,padx=5,pady=5)

# creating a label for minutes and attaching it the main
    window

lbl_mins= Label(main_window, text
    ="Minutes",bg="#6699ff",fg="#595959", font=("Courier",14))
lbl_mins.grid(row=2, column=2,padx=5,pady=5)

# creating a label for seconds and attaching it the main
    window
lbl_sec= Label(main_window, text
    ="Seconds",bg="#6699ff",fg="#595959", font=("Courier",14))
lbl_sec.grid(row=2, column=3,padx=5,pady=5)
```

The following script adds three text fields using Entry widgets. The values for hours, minutes and seconds for the alarm are entered in these text fields.

**Script 6:**

```
# creating a text field for hours and #attaching it to the main
    window
txt_hours=StringVar()
tf_hours=ttk.Entry(main_window,textvariable=txt_hours)
tf_hours.grid(row=3, column=1,padx=15,pady=15)

# creating a text field for minutes and #attaching it to the
    main window
txt_mins=StringVar()
tf_mins=ttk.Entry(main_window,textvariable=txt_mins)
tf_mins.grid(row=3, column=2,padx=15,pady=15)

# creating a text field for minutes and #attaching it to the
    main window
txt_sec=StringVar()
tf_se=ttk.Entry(main_window,textvariable=txt_sec)
tf_se.grid(row=3, column=3,padx=15,pady=15)
```

Before you add a button for setting the alarm, you need to define a callback function that contains the logic used to set the alarm. The following script implements that function.

In the set_alarm() function of the following script, the values from the hours, minutes, and seconds text fields are read and stored in the alarm_time variable. The format of the time is hh:mm:ss.

Next, after every second, it is checked whether the alarm time is equal to the current time or not. If the alarm time is equal to the current time, an audio file "siren.wav" is played using the PlaySound() method from the winsound module. You can find the "siren.wav" file in the resources folder. You can also play any other audio file if you want.

**Script 7:**

```
def set_alarm():


    while True:
        # Set Alarm
        alarm_time = f"{txt_hours.get()}:{txt_mins.
    get()}:{txt_mins.get()}"

        # get current time after every 1 second
        time.sleep(1)

        # get time in hours minutes and seconds format
        current_time = datetime.datetime.now().
    strftime("%H:%M:%S")

        # print current time in a text field
        txt_ct.set(current_time)

        # Check if current system time is equal to the alarm
    time
        if current_time == alarm_time:

            # playing sound
            winsound.PlaySound('E:/Datasets/siren.wav',
    winsound.SND_FILENAME | winsound.SND_ASYNC)
```

Next, you run the set_alarm() method inside a thread. To do so, you create a method start_alarm_thread(). Inside the start_alarm_thread() method, you create an object of the Thread class and pass the name of the set_alarm method as the parameter value to the target parameter. To start the thread, you call the start() method.

If you directly call the set_alarm() method, your GUI will not be responsive. If you run the set_alarm() method inside the thread, the set_alarm() method will execute in parallel with other GUI operations, and your main window will not become unresponsive.

**Script 8:**

```
def start_alarm_thread():
    t1=Thread(target = set_alarm)
    t1.start()
```

Next, you will create the button, which, when clicked, will execute the set_alarm() method in a thread. You can see that the callback function for the button in the following script is start_alarm_thread().

**Script 9:**

```
# creating a button for setting an alarm and attaching it to
    the main window
btn_Set_alarm = Button(main_window,
        text = "SET ALARM",
        bg = "#ff9966",
        fg = "#595959",
        font = ("Courier", 14),
        command = start_alarm_thread)

btn_Set_alarm.grid(row=4, column=1, columnspan=3, padx=5,
    pady=5)
```

Finally, the following script adds a label and a text field that displays the current system time.

**Script 10:**

```
# creating a label for seconds and attaching it the main
   window
lbl_ct= Label(main_window, text ="Current
   time",bg="#6699ff",fg="#595959", font=("Courier",10))
lbl_ct.grid(row=5, column=1,padx=5,pady=5)

# creating a text field for minutes and attaching it to the
   main window
txt_ct=StringVar()
tf_ct=ttk.Entry(main_window,textvariable=txt_ct, width=20)
tf_ct.grid(row=5, column=2,padx=15,pady=15)
```

**Script 11:**

```
# displaying the main window
main_window.mainloop()
```

### Final Output

If you execute all the scripts in this project, you will see the following output. Try to enter hours, minutes, and seconds in the corresponding text fields to set the alarm, and then click the SET ALARM button. You will hear a siren when the current system time becomes equal to the alarm time.

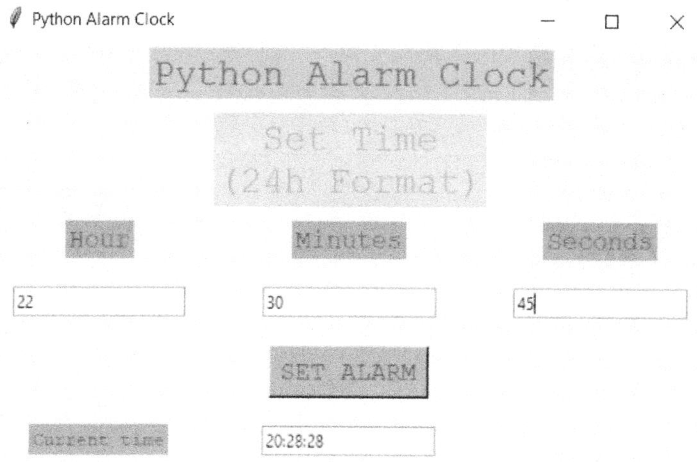

## Project 3

# Hangman Game in Python

In this project, you will see how to create a very basic version of the hangman game.

In the hangman game, a user has to guess a word. At each step of the game, the user guesses as to whether or not a particular character exists in the word. If that character exists in the word, the character is entered at its position in the word. Else, if a guess is wrong, the number of the remaining allowed wrong guesses decreases by 1. A user can make only a limited number of wrong guesses. If a user can guess the word before the number of allowed wrong guesses, the user wins; else, he loses.

Let's see how to develop such a game with Python. The GUI of the game will look like this:

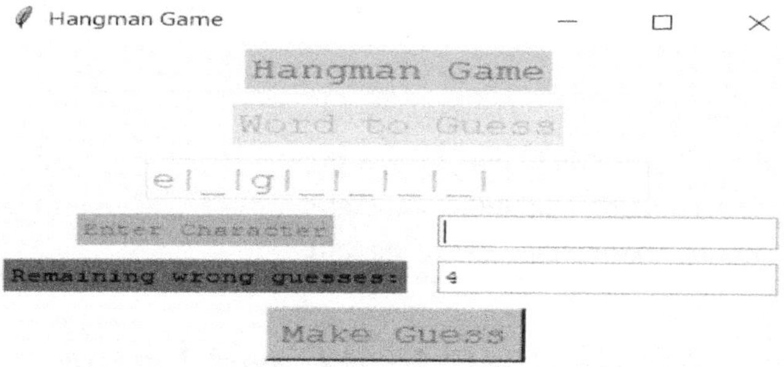

## Importing the Required Libraries

As always, you start by importing the required libraries.

**Script 1:**

```
# importing tkinter
from tkinter import *

# importing tkk
from tkinter import ttk

import random

# importing showinfor message box
from tkinter.messagebox import showinfo
```

## Creating Main Window

Next, you create the main window.

**Script 2:**

```
main_window = Tk()
main_window.title("Hangman Game")
main_window.geometry("400x400+100+200")
```

The following script adds three columns to your main window.

**Script 3:**

```
# adding three columns to main window
main_window.columnconfigure(0, weight=1)
main_window.columnconfigure(1, weight=1)
main_window.columnconfigure(2, weight=1)
```

## Adding Widgets and Logic

The following script adds two labels in the first and second rows of your main window. The first label displays the title

*Hangman Game*. The second label displays the text *Word to Guess.*

The following script also adds a text field using the Entry widget. This text field contains dashes for each character in the word to be guessed. Whenever a character is correctly guessed by the user, the dash in the corresponding position of the text field is replaced by the character guessed correctly.

**Script 4:**

```
# creating a label for title and attaching it the main window
my_label= Label(main_window, text ="Hangman
    Game",bg="#b3b3b3",fg="#ff3300", font=("Courier",15))
my_label.grid(row=0, column=0,columnspan=3,padx=5,pady=5)


# creating a label for a message and attaching it the main
    window
my_labe2 = Label(main_window, text ="Word to
    Guess",bg="#cccccc",fg="#3399ff", font=("Courier",15))
my_labe2.grid(row=1, column=0,columnspan=3,padx=5,pady=5)

# creating a text field for empty string and attaching it the
    main window
txt_word=StringVar()
tf_word=ttk.Entry(main_window,textvariable=txt_word,
    font=("Courier",15), state='disabled')
tf_word.grid(row=2, column=0,columnspan=3,padx=2,pady=5)
```

The following script initializes some of the variables that we are going to use to develop the hangman game. The script contains the initialize_values() method, which assigns default values to the variables.

The words list stores the names of all the words. The word that is to be guessed will be randomly selected from this list. You can add more words if you like.

The rem_guess will store the integer value for the number of remaining guesses. The value of this variable is initially set to 5. You can add or decrease this value if you want.

The cor_guess variable stores the number of correctly guessed characters. The value of this variable is set to 0 by default.

The empty_str variable will hold the empty string displaying dashes in the text field. Each dash is separated by a vertical bar.

Finally, the original_word variable stores the original word in a format where each character is separated by a vertical bar. This variable is created so that when a user correctly guesses a character, the index of that character can be fetched from the original_word string. The character guessed will be replaced in the empty_str at that particular index.

**Script 5:**

```
# list of words (you can add more words if you want)
words = "kite", "table", "mathematics", "english", "fabulous",
   "difficult"

word_to_guess = ""
rem_guess = ""
cor_guess = ""
empty_str = ""
original_word = ""

def initialize_values():

    global word_to_guess
    global original_word
    global empty_str
    global rem_guess
    global cor_guess
```

```
    print("helllo =========")
    # randomly selecting the word to guess
    word_to_guess = random.choice(words)

    # setting default number of remaining wrong guesses
    rem_guess = 5

    # setting the default number of correct guesses
    cor_guess = 0

    # empty string to display on GUI
    empty_str = ""

    # string which keeps track of character indexes
    original_word = ""

    for char in word_to_guess:
        empty_str = empty_str + "_|"
        original_word = original_word + char + "|"

    txt_word.set(empty_str)

# intitializing values
initialize_values()
```

The following script creates two labels and two text fields. The user enters the character to be guessed in the first text field. The second text field displays the allowed number of remaining wrong guesses.

**Script 6:**

```
# creating a label for input character
lbl_ip= Label(main_window, text ="Enter
   Character",bg="#6699ff",fg="#595959", font=("Courier",10))
lbl_ip.grid(row=3, column=0,padx=5,pady=5)

# creating a text field for input characters and attaching it
   to the main window
```

```
txt_ip=StringVar()
tf_ip=ttk.Entry(main_window,textvariable=txt_ip,
    font=("Courier",10))
tf_ip.grid(row=3, column=1,padx=5,pady=5)

# creating a label for remaining guesses

# creating a label for input character
lbl_rg= Label(main_window, text ="Remaining wrong
    guesses:",bg="red",fg="black", font=("Courier",10))
lbl_rg.grid(row=4, column=0,padx=5,pady=5)

# creating a text field for remaining wrong guesses and
    attaching it to the main window
txt_rg=StringVar()
txt_rg.set(rem_guess)#setting remaining wrong guesses to the
    default value

tf_rg=ttk.Entry(main_window,textvariable=txt_rg,
    font=("Courier",10))
tf_rg.grid(row=4, column=1,padx=5,pady=5)
```

Before you define a button to make a guess, let's define the main logic for the game.

The following script defines the make_guess() function that is used as a callback when a user enters a character and clicks the *Make Guess* button (which will be created in the next script).

Inside the main_guess() method, you first access various variables that you defined in Script 5. You also access the text field for user input.

If a user enters 0 or more than 1 character in the input text field, a message is displayed that he/she can only enter 1 character.

Next, if the character entered by the user is not found in the word to be guessed, the allowed number of remaining wrong guesses is decremented by 1. Two possibilities are checked after that.

(i) If the allowed number of remaining wrong guesses becomes 0, a message is displayed that the user lost the game, and he should try again. The intitialize_values() method is called to rest all the variable values. Also, the values for the input text field and the text field containing the allowed number of wrong guesses are reset.

(ii) If the allowed number of remaining wrong guesses is not equal to 0, that means the user has more chances to guess the word. In that case, a message is displayed that a user made a wrong guess, and the game continues.

In case a user makes a correct guess regarding a character, there are two possible scenarios:

(i) It is checked if the number of correct guesses is equal to the number of characters in the word to be guessed. If this is the case, a message is displayed to the user that he/she won the game. The intitialize_values() method is called to rest all the variable values. Also, the values for the input text field and the text field containing the allowed number of wrong guesses are reset. The user can again play the game.

(ii) If the number of correct guesses and the number of characters in the word are not equal, the guessed character replaces the dash in the empty string. The input text field is set to contain an empty string, and the value of the allowed number of wrong guesses is decremented by 1.

Here is the script for the make_guess() method:

## Script 7:

```
def make_guess():

    # accessing global variables
    global word_to_guess
    global original_word
    global empty_str
    global rem_guess
    global cor_guess
    global txt_ip

    # if the input string is empty or contains 2 characters
    if (txt_ip.get() == "") or (len(txt_ip.get()) > 1):
        showinfo(
            title = "Information",
            message = "Input Cannot be Empty or more than one
character"
            )
        return
    input_char = txt_ip.get()

    # if the input character exists in the word to be guessed
    if input_char not in word_to_guess:
        txt_ip.set("")
        rem_guess = rem_guess - 1
        txt_rg.set(rem_guess)

        # if no remaining wrong guess
        if rem_guess == 0:

            showinfo(
            title = "Information",
            message = "You have used all your guesses. \n You
lost. \n The correct word is: " + word_to_guess +". \n Try
Again"
            )
            initialize_values()
            txt_ip.set("")
            txt_rg.set(rem_guess)
```

```
        # if you have more wrong guesses left
        else:
            showinfo(
            title = "Information",
            message = "Wrong Guess"
            )


        return

    # if the input character exists in the word to be guessed
    else:

        cor_guess = cor_guess + 1
        #if the number of correct guesses are equal to the
word length
        if cor_guess == len(word_to_guess):

            showinfo(title = "Information", message =
"Congratulations, You Won! \n  Play Again")
            initialize_values()
            txt_ip.set("")
            txt_rg.set(rem_guess)

        # if the guess is correct but still there are
        # characters left to be guessed
        else:
            position = original_word.index(input_char)
            empty_str = empty_str[:position] + input_char +
empty_str[position + 1:]
            txt_word.set(empty_str)
            txt_ip.set("")
```

The following script creates a button titled *Make Guess*. Clicking this button calls the make_guess() method.

### Script 8:

```
# creating a  button for setting an alarm and attaching it to
    the main window
btn_check_char= Button(main_window,
                        text ="Make Guess",
bg="#ff9966",
fg="#595959",
                        font=("Courier",14),
                        command =make_guess
)

btn_check_char.grid(row=5,column=0,columnspan=3,padx=5,
    pady=5)
```

Execute the following script to keep the main window visible.

### Script 9:

```
# displaying the main window
main_window.mainloop()
```

### Final Output

Here is the final output of your project. You can see from the following screenshot that the user has guessed two characters, "e" and "g," correctly. Also, the user has made one wrong guess since the allowed number of remaining wrong guesses is 4.

And that's it. You have developed your very own hangman game. Congratulations!

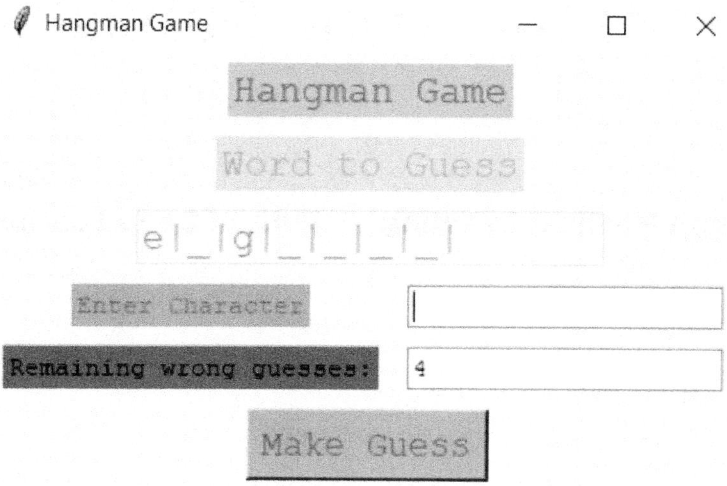
Hangman Game
Hangman Game
Word to Guess
e|_|g|_|_|_|_|
Enter Character
Remaining wrong guesses:
4
Make Guess

**Data Science with Python**

https://bit.ly/3wVQ5iN

**Statistics with Python**

https://bit.ly/3z27KHt

# Exercise Solutions

## Exercise 2.1

**Question 1:**

To write a multi-line string, you need to wrap a string in:

A. Double Quotes
B. Triple Quotes
C. Single Quote
D. None of the Above

**Answer: B**

**Question 2:**

The following function can be used to add an item to a tuple:

A. add()
B. insert()
C. append()
D. None of the Above

**Answer: D**

**Question 3:**

What will be the output of the following code?

```
colors = {"color1":"red",
          "color2": "blue",
          "color1": "green"}

print(colors["color1"])
```

A. Red

B. Blue

C. Green

D. None of the Above

**Answer: A**

## Exercise 2.2

Create a dictionary that contains days of a week (starting from Monday) as values. The keys should start from 1 with an increment of 1. Display the 3rd week of the day using its key. Use a loop to display all the key-value pairs (see the section on accessing dictionary items for reference).

**Solution:**

```
days = {1:"Monday",
        2:"Tuesday",
        3:"Wednesday",
        4:"Thursday",
        5:"Friday",
        6:"Saturday",
        7:"Sunday"}

print(days[3])

for k,v in days.items():
    print(str(k)+" ->"+v)
```

# Exercise 3.1

**Question 1:**

What will be the outcome of the following code?

```
a =["red","green","blue"]
print("red" is in a)
```

A. True

B. False

C. SyntaxError

D. red is in a

**Answer: C**

**Question 2:**

What will be the outcome of the following code?

```
X =100
Y =50

not(X is Y)
```

A. True

B. False

C. SyntaxError

D. None of the Above

**Answer: A**

**Question 3:**

Which of the following membership operators are supported by Python?

A. In

B. Out

C. Not In

D. Both A and C

**Answer: D**

## Exercise 3.2

Suppose you have the following the following three Python variables:

```
a =400
b =350
c = b
d =[100,200,300,400]
```

Perform the following tasks:

1. Show the output of a greater than b
2. Apply and operator between two logical conditions: (1) b is smaller than a, and (ii) c is b.
3. Check if b in d
4. Check if a in d
5. Check if a + b is not in d

**Solution:**

```
a = 400
b = 350
c = b
d = [100,200,300,400]

print(a > b)
print(b < a and b is c)
print(b in d)
print(a in d)
print((a + b) not in d)
```

## Exercise 4.1

**Question 1:**

You should use a *while* loop when:

A. You want to repeatedly execute a code until a certain condition returns true

B. When you know the exact number of times you want to execute a piece of code

C. To execute a code 10 times

D. None of the above

**Answer: A**

**Question 2:**

A loop defined inside another loop is called an:

A. Inner Loop

B. Nested Loop

C. Both A and B

D. None of the above

**Answer: C**

**Question 3:**

The continue statement is used in loops to:

A. Break out of the loop

B. Move to the next line of the code

C. Go back to the beginning of a loop

D. Skip two lines of code

**Answer: C**

## Exercise 4.2

Write a program that prints the prime numbers between 1 and 100.

**Solution:**

```
for i in range(1, 101):
    if i == 1:
        print(i)
    else:
        prime = True
        for j in range(2,i):
            if i % j == 0:
                prime = False
                break
            if prime:
                print(i)
```

# Exercise 5.1

**Question 1:**

A Python function can return:

A. a single value

B. multiple values

C. functions

D. all of the above

**Answer: D**

**Question 2:**

You can define multiple expressions in a lambda function using:

A. lists

B. tuples

C. dictionaries

D. None of the Above

**Answer: B**

**Question 3:**

A nested function defined inside an outer function can be?

A. accessed only inside the outer function

B. accessed anywhere in the code

C. accessed in the same class

D. all of the above

**Answer: A**

## Exercise 5.2

Write a function that calculates and prints the first N numbers of the Fibonacci series, where N is any integer.

In Fibonacci series, the next number is the sum of the previous two numbers for example:

1 = 1 = 1

2 = 1 + 0 = 1

3 = 1 + 1 = 2

4 = 2 + 1 = 3

5 = 3 + 2 = 5

6 = 5 + 3 = 8

7 = 8 + 5 = 13

8 = 13 + 8 = 21

**Solution:**

```
def get_fib(num):
    if num == 1 or num == 2:
        return 1
    else:
        return get_fib(num-1) + get_fib(num-2)

get_fib(8)
```

# Exercise 6.1

**Question 1:**

What is true for Python:

A. A child can inherit from only one parent class

B. A parent class can only have one child class

C. A child class can inherit from multiple parent classes

D. None of the Above

**Answer: D**

**Question 2:**

An instance method can be accessed via:

A. class name

B. class and object names

C. object name

D. All of the above

**Answer: C**

**Question 3:**

Which of the following method is used to call the parent class constructor in Python?

A. parent()

B. base()

C. super()

D. object()

**Answer: C**

# Exercise 6.2

Perform the following tasks:

1. Create a Parent class Vehicle with two instance attributes: name and price, and one instance method show_vehicle(). The show_vehicle() method displays the name and price attributes.
2. Initialize the Vehicle class attributes using a constructor.
3. Create a class Car that inherits the Parent Vehicle class. Add an attribute named tires to the Car class. Override the show_vehicle() method of the parent Vehicle class and display name, price, and tire attributes.
4. Inside the Car class constructor, call the Vehicle class constructor and pass the name and price to the parent Vehicle class constructor.
5. Create objects of Car and Vehicle classes, and call show_vehicle() method using both objects.

**Solution:**

```
class Vehicle:

    def __init__(self, name, price):
        self.name = name
        self.price = price

    def show_vehicle(self):
        print("The vehicle name is:", self.name)
        print("The vehicle price is:", str(self.price))

class Car(Vehicle):

    def __init__(self, name, price, tires):
        super().__init__(name, price)
        self.tires = tires
```

```
    def show_vehicle(self):
        print("The vehicle name is:", self.name)
        print("The vehicle price is:", str(self.price))
        print("Number of tyres:", str(self.tires))

vehicle = Vehicle("Vehicle", 20000)
vehicle.show_vehicle()

print("=====")

car = Car("Car", 15000, 4)
car.show_vehicle()
```

# Exercise 7.1

**Question 1:**

What is the minimum number of try and except blocks required to catch all the exceptions in Python?

A. 1
B. Equal to the number of all exceptions in Python
C. 2
D. None of the Above

**Answer: A**

**Question 2:**

To create a user-defined exception, you have to create a class that inherits from the following class:

A. Error
B. Exception
C. Try
D. Catch

**Answer: B**

**Question 3:**

Exception handling is important because it:

A. Saves your program from crashing at runtime
B. Helps display custom messages to the user in case of an error
C. Speeds up program execution
D. Both A and B

**Answer: D**

## Exercise 7.2

Create a custom exception named EvenNumberInsertionException, which tells users that they cannot add an even number in a list of integers. Create a list and add some odd and even numbers to it. Raise the EvenNumberInsertionException and tell the user the even number added along with the error message.

**Solution:**

```
class EvenNumberInsertionException(Exception):
    """Exception raised when an even number is inserted in a
list

    Attributes:
        new_list -- the list itself
        error_message -- the detail of the exception
    """

    def __init__(self, new_list, error_message="Exception: The
list cannot contain an even number"):
        self.new_list = new_list
        self.error_message = error_message
        super().__init__(self.error_message)
```

```
    def __str__(self):
        return f'{self.new_list[-1]} -> {self.error_message}'


my_list = []

for i in [1,3,5,7,8,9,12,15,17]:

    my_list.append(i)
    print(my_list)
    if i%2 == 0:
        raise EvenNumberInsertionException(my_list)
```

# Exercise 8.1

**Question 1:**

The value of "w" for mode attribute in the open() function:

A. Opens a file for writing
B. Creates a new file if a file with the same name doesn't exist
C. Overwrites all the contents of an existing file
D. All of the above

**Answer: D**

**Question 2:**

Which method of the csv.write object is used for adding a single record to a CSV file?

A. addrows()
B. writerows()
C. appendrows()
D. insertrows()

**Answer: B**

**Question 3:**

What are the parameters values that you need to pass to the connect() method of the socket()to connect to a remote server application through a socket?

A. Server name and server ip name

B. Server ip address and port number

C. Server ip address, port number, and application name

D. Both A and C

**Answer: B**

## Exercise 8.2

Create a new text file. Write three lines of text in the text file. Read all the text from the file line by line using the `with` operator.

**Solution:**

```
file_handle_text=open("E:/Datasets/my_new_file.txt","w")
file_handle_text.write("This is line 1\n")
file_handle_text.write("This is line 2\n")
file_handle_text.write("This is line 3\n")
file_handle_text.close()

withopen("E:/Datasets/my_new_file.txt", mode ='r')asfile_handle_
    text:
file_content=file_handle_text.read()
print(file_content)
```

# Exercise 9.1

**Question 1:**

The pattern '(\Ag)|(\d+)' matches

A. All the digits

B. The strings with characters Ag

C. Strings that start with g or which are digits

D. All of the above

**Answer: C**

**Question 2:**

In Python, the function used to replace a string with another string is:

A. replace()

B. sub()

C. substitute()

D. rep()

**Answer: B**

**Question 3:**

The escape character used to escape meta characters within a regex pattern is:

A. Forward slash

B. Backslash

C. Alteration

D. Escape

**Answer: B**

# Exercise 9.2

Write a regular expression that returns all words from a list that contain a carrot (^) symbol or a dollar sign ($), or a plus (+) sign.

**Solution:**

```
import re

pattern = '(.*\^.*)|(.*\$.*)|(.*\+.*)'
string_list = ["path+ology", "biolo$gy", "25", ""
   "geogr^aphy", "psychology", "mathematics"]

for str in string_list:
    result = re.match(pattern, str)
    if result:
        print(str)
```

# Exercise 10.1

**Question 1:**

Which command is used to close the Python debugger?

A. quit

B. close

C. q

D. c

**Answer: C**

**Question 2:**

The following expression is used to specify a default value to default dictionaries in Python:

A. defaultdictionary(lambda: "value")
B. defaultdict(lambda = "value")
C. DefaultDict(lambda : "value")
D. none of the above

**Answer: D**

**Question 3:**

Which of the following modules and expressions can be used to find script time in Jupyter?

A. ##
B. timeit
C. time
D. all of the above

**Answer: D**

## Exercise 10.2

Find the number of counts for each unique value in the following list using the *for* loop and the Counter object `[Apple, Orange, Apple, Apple, Orange, Banana, Orange, Orange]`.

**Solution:**

```
fruits = ["Apple","Orange","Apple","Apple","Orange","Banana",
    "Orange","Orange"]

# Solution using for loop

fruits_dic = {}
```

```
for fruit in fruits:
    if fruit not in fruits_dic:
        fruits_dic[fruit] = 1
    else:
        fruits_dic[fruit] +=1

print(fruits_dic)


from collections import Counter

fruits_count = Counter(fruits)
print(fruits_count)
```

## Exercise 11.1

**Question 1:**

To create a custom module in Python, you need to create:

A. an object

B. a Python file

C. a class

D. a function

**Answer: B**

**Question 2:**

To create a class in a custom module, you need to:

A. a keyword mymodule

B. add a keyword module

C. add a keyword module class

D. none of the above

**Answer: D**

**Question 3:**

In python, you can have __ levels for module dependencies:

A. unlimited

B. 1

C. 2

D. 3

**Answer: D**

## Exercise 11.2

Perform the following tasks:

Create a custom module1 that contains a function that returns the cube of a number.

Create a custom module2 that imports module 1 and contains a function that returns the sum of cubes of two numbers.

Import module1 and module2 and first find the cube of a number, and then find the sum of cubes of two numbers.

**Solution:**

```
# code for module1

def find_cube(num):
return num * num * num

# code for module2

import module1

def find_sum_cube(num1, num2):
    num1_cube1 = (module1.find_cube(num1))
    num1_cube2 = (module1.find_cube(num2))

return num1_cube1 + num1_cube2
```

```
# code for test file

import module1
import module2

result = module1.find_cube(3)
    print(result)

result = module2.find_sum_cube(2,3)
    print(result)
```

## Exercise 12.1

**Question 1:**

You need to call the mainloop() method from the object of the Tk class in Tkinter because:

A. It opens the main GUI window
B. It keeps the GUI window open
C. It allows users to interact with widgets
D. None of the above

**Answer: B**

**Question 2:**

Which method is used to display a message box in Tkinter?

A. showmessage()
B. displaymessage()
C. showinfo()
D. displayinfo()

**Answer: C**

**Question 3:**

What is the distance of the Tkinter window drawn using the geometry method geometry("500x500+100+300") from the top of the screen?

A. 500

B. 100

C. 200

D. 300

**Answer: D**

## Exercise 12.2

Create a simple login form that looks like the one in the following image, using Tkinter.

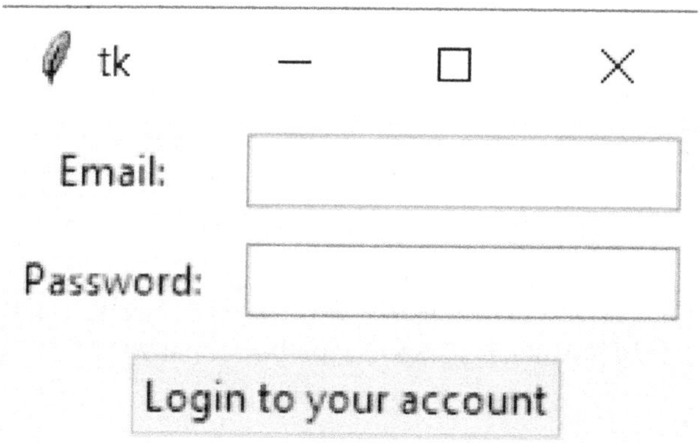


When you click the `Login to your account` button, the email should be displayed in a message box.

**Solution:**

```
from tkinter import *
from tkinter import ttk


main_window = Tk()


main_window.columnconfigure(0, weight=1)
main_window.columnconfigure(1, weight=1)


email_label = ttk.Label(main_window,  text = "Email:" )
email_label.grid(column=0, row=0, padx=5, pady=5)


email_text = StringVar()
email_field = ttk.Entry(main_window, textvariable = email_text)
email_field.grid(column=1, row=0, padx=5, pady=5)


pass_label = ttk.Label(main_window,  text = "Password:" )
pass_label.grid(column=0, row=1, padx=5, pady=5)


pass_text = StringVar()
pass_field = ttk.Entry(main_window, textvariable = pass_text)
pass_field.grid(column=1, row=1, padx=5, pady=5)


def my_func():

    text = ""
    if email_text.get() == "":
        text = "Enter your email first"
    else:
        text = "Your email is:" + email_text.get()
```

```
    showinfo(title = "Information", message = text)


# creating a themed button
my_button2 = ttk.Button(main_window,
                        text = "Login to your account",
                        command = my_func
                        )

# attaching a button to first row and third  column
my_button2.grid(column=0, row=2, columnspan = 2, padx=5,
pady=5)


main_window.mainloop()
```

## Exercise 13.1

**Question 1:**

Which NumPy function is used for the element-wise multiplication of two matrices?

A. np.dot(matrix1, matrix2)

B. np.multiply(matrix1, matrix2)

C. np.elementwise(matrix1, matrix2)

D. None of the above

**Answer: B**

**Question 2:**

Which function is used to sort Pandas dataframe by a column value?

A. sort_dataframe()

B. sort_rows()

C. sort_values()

D. sort_records()

**Answer: C**

**Question 3:**

How to show percentage values on a Matplotlib pie chart?

A. autopct = '%1.1f%%'

B. percentage = '%1.1f%%'

C. perc = '%1.1f%%'

D. None of the above

**Answer: A**

## Exercise 13.2

Create a random NumPy array of 5 rows and 4 columns. Using array indexing and slicing, display the items from row 3 to end and column 2 to end.

**Solution:**

```
uniform_random=np.random.rand(4,5)
print(uniform_random)
print("Result")
print(uniform_random[2:,3:])
```

Made in the USA
Monee, IL
05 November 2026

67816238R00213